HERMANN COHEN

HERMANN COHEN
The Challenge of a Religion of Reason

by
William Kluback

Scholars Press
Chico, California

HERMANN COHEN
The Challenge
of a Religion of Reason

by
William Kluback

Library of Congress Cataloging in Publication Data
Kluback, William.
Hermann Cohen : the challenge of a religion
of reason.

(Brown Judaic studies ; 53)
Bibliography: p.
1. Cohen, Hermann, 1842–1918. I. Title. II. Series.
B3216.C74K65 1984 170'.92'4 83-14147
ISBN 0-89130-645-5

Printed in the United States of America

This book is dedicated to the memory
of my teacher and friend
Samuel Hugo Bergmann

WILLIAM KLUBACK is Professor of Philosophy at Kingsborough Community College at the City University of New York.

CONTENTS

INTRODUCTION

This study of Hermann Cohen is undertaken to show that from 1907 to 1918 a *Weltanschauung*, dominated by Kant, was surpassed by one which embodied a faith in the truth of Israel's monotheism. It is necessary to see a continuity in Cohen's thought with the Kantian tradition but, at the same time, to be aware that new elements were being introduced, new emphases and new evaluations were being made. Cohen's thought always bore a religiosity, although it did not express at first a particular religious attitude or use a specific religious vocabulary. There are changes in direction; these do not necessarily imply radical breaks. Cohen's Kantian background is the decisive factor in his later move toward a more concrete embracing of Judaism, of the co-relationship between man and God. Ethics remained, however, the fundamental basis of his *Lebenserfarung*. This study stresses the importance of viewing Cohen's thought from the point of view of a *Lebenserfarung*. In Cohen's thought there is a systematic evaluation of what he considered to be the major trends of European philosophy; his affirmations and rejections give birth to values that place his philosophy within the great tradition of Western European ethics: Kant's exposition of the moral law. The vital role of Judaism in this history of Western philosophy is explored and commented upon with imagination and profundity. The uniqueness of Cohen's achievement is the object of this book.

The thought of every great seminal thinker necessitates a reconsideration of the eternal problems of philosophy. Cohen's thought is a powerful evaluation of these problems; a confrontation with Cohen's ideas forces us to rethink the perennial adventure of philosophy into these realms which surpass the understanding and which belong to the realm of thought, to the reason in which the eternal ideas of God, immortality, and freedom find their source. Never before in the history of thought have philosophy and Judaism come so close. Cohen's attempt to bring together the visions of the prophets with Kant's moral law and the awe that it inspires, the sublimity which it evokes in us, should impose upon us a task to continuously seek in religion that universality which philosophy comprehends and embraces as the law of humanity experienced as freedom.

Chapter I

THE BACKGROUND: KANT'S DOCTRINE OF VIRTUES

The autonomous creativity of reason, the lyric of prayer, the ethical philosophy of Kant, and the prophecy of Ezekiel are apparent contradictory articulations of experience. Hermann Cohen gave his life to that vast endeavor of joining a Kantian ethic to a biblical faith.

Cohen was born in 1842 in Coswig, Anhalt, near the town of Dessau, the birthplace of the Jewish philosopher Moses Mendelssohn (1729–86). The Jewish life of Coswig centered around Cohen's father, who was both cantor and Hebrew teacher. The parents intended their son for the Rabbinate. From 1857 to 1861 Cohen studied at the Jewish Theological Seminary in Breslau. There he studied with some of the great men of German Jewish scholarship: Graetz, Joel, Frankel, and Bernays.[1] After four years of further study at the Universities of Breslau and Berlin, Cohen yielded to the philosophical gadfly and in 1865 took his doctorate.[2]

It was, however, in 1871 with the publication of *Kant's Theory of Experience* (*Kants Theorie der Erfahrung*) that Cohen's professional career began. The book marked the direction that he was to take in his Kant interpretation and made possible his appointment as *Privatdozent* in the University of Marburg in 1873.[3] This direction remained unchanged, for shortly before his death in 1918 Cohen had written a third preface reaffirming the critical idealism which the book expounded and the pivotal role of Kant's ethics in the history of man's search for a meaningful concept of humanity and peace.[4]

[1] Hermann Cohen, "Ein Gruss der Pietaet an das Breslauer Seminar" (1904), in *Juedische Schriften* (Berlin, 1924), II, 418–24.

[2] Theses: *Philosophorum de antinomia necessitates et contingentiae doctrinae*. In Hermann Cohen, *Schriften zur Philosophie und Zeitgeschichte* (Berlin, 1928), I, 1–29. See Cohen's *Vita*, p. 28.

[3] Henry Dussort, *L'Ecole de Marburg* (Paris, 1963). This book provides a valuable survey of German philosophy attempting to come to terms with Kant. Particular emphasis is given to the School of Marburg.

[4] Hermann Cohen, *Kants Theorie der Erfahrung*, 3d ed. (Berlin, 1925), xxi. "Die Zuversicht, dass wie Deutschland nicht untergehen, nicht erniedrigt und nicht verringert werden darf, so auch der Geist der deutschen Philosophie, der Geist Kants in seiner

With the support of F. A. Lange, the author of *The History of Materialism*, Cohen came to Marburg. The second edition of the *Theory of Experience* (1885) was dedicated to Lange. After Lange's death in 1876, Cohen became full professor and remained at the university until 1912. Cohen defined his Judaism similar to Lange's definition of Protestantism. This was the basis of their friendship. Cohen on several occasions wrote about Lange (1876, 1893, 1914) and provided a critical introduction to the ninth edition of *The History of Materialism*.[5] Although Cohen's work at Marburg was an almost exhaustive attempt to display the pure power of reason and its limits, an undercurrent of religious longing was present. This is more readily apparent in Cohen's letters[6] and in the testimony of Cohen's close friend at Marburg, the Protestant theologian Wilhelm Herrmann.[7]

Cohen's first works were three interpretative studies of Kant's systematic philosophy; they dealt with the theory of knowledge, the foundation of ethics, and the foundation of aesthetics. These works appeared over a period of 18 years from 1871 to 1889.[8] Cohen was not only a commentator on Kant's philosophical texts, but a system builder in his own right. This system can be dated from 1883, when *The Principle of the Infinitesimal and Its History* saw light.[9] The titles of the volumes which comprise the system, insofar as each has the word *pure* in it, indicate that the principle of the infinitesimal is realized in each of its systematic parts. The volumes are: (1) *Logic of Pure Knowledge*, (2) *Ethics of the Pure Will*, and (3) *Aesthetics of the Pure Feeling*.[10]

Apart from innumerable articles and studies devoted to the history of philosophic thought from Plato to Maimonides, from Galileo to Leibniz,

---

geschichtlichen Ewigkeit die Menschheit zum wahrhaften Frieden der Humanitaet, zur Vereinigung im Geiste bringen wird."

5 See the following articles: "Friedrich Albert Lange, Nachruf" (1876); "Friedrich Albert Lange" (1893); Einleitung mit kritischem Nachtrag zu Lange's "Geschichte des Materialismus" (1914); see *Schriften zur Philosophie und Zeitgegeschichte* (Berlin, 1928), vol. II.

6 Hermann Cohen, *Briefe*, ed. Bertha and Bruno Strauss (Berlin, 1939). See in particular Cohen's letters to his friend and fellow philosopher August Stadler, Marburg, Jan. 17, 1890, pp. 64–66.

7 Wilhelm Herrmann, "Christliche Welt," March 1907, p. 227. This review was the second of a two-part review of Cohen's *Ethik des reinen Willens*.

8 Hermann Cohen, *Kants Theorie der Erfahrung*, 1871; *Kants Begruendung der Ethik*, 1877; *Kants Begruendung der Aesthetik*, 1889.

9 *Das Prinzip der Infinitesimalmethode und seine Geschichte*, in *Schriften zur Philosophie und Zeitgeschichte*, vol. II. See S. H. Bergman, *The Philosophy of Solomon Maimon* (Jerusalem 1967), Chap. XIV, pp. 256–71, for an important discussion of Cohen's relation to Maimon and the commonality of their sources relating to principles of the infinitesimal. Bergman indicates the sources to be both Leibniz and Lazarus ben David.

10 *Logik der reinen Erkenntnis* (1902); *Ethik des reinen Willens* (1904); *Aesthetik des reinen Gefuehles* (1912).

Cohen was never distant from Jewish studies and concerns. These writings compose five volumes and are indispensable sources of this thought.[11]

In 1915 Cohen published a book dedicated to the Marburg School, *The Concept of Religion in the System of Philosophy*,[12] the consequences of which seem to threaten the unity and singularity of his previous approach to philosophy. Wilhelm Herrmann had already indicated in 1907 that Cohen had not properly dealt with the religious. This book and Cohen's final treatise, *Religion of Reason from the Sources of Judaism*,[13] can in some way be considered both as an answer to Herrmann's criticism and a consequence of Cohen's deepening involvement in Jewish affairs from 1912 to 1918. It was in this period that Cohen, no longer in Marburg but in Berlin, traveled to the Jewish communities of Poland and Russia in 1914 and lectured at the "Hochschule fuer die Wissenschaft des Judentums." The emphasis of these six years becomes evident when we consider the discussion of the virtues first in the *Ethics of the Pure Will* and then in the *Religion of Reason*. The first book ends with humanity as the highest expression of the harmony of virtues and the source of moral feeling; the second book concludes with a chapter on peace which unfolds the messianic hope of mankind and points to the eternal task of man's historical existence. There appears to have been a shift in Cohen's thought. The doctrine of the virtues, their elaboration by Kant in the second part of the *Metaphysics of Morals* and then by Cohen in the *Ethics of the Pure Will* and the *Religion of Reason*, the changes in emphases, the omissions and additions provide a way to understand the shifting relationship between ethics and religion.

The criticism of Cohen's Marburg colleague, Herrmann, previously mentioned, deserves close attention because it points to serious inadequacies in Cohen's treatment of religion. More important than the attempt to prove the strong influence of Protestantism on Cohen is the concrete and decisive analysis that Wilhelm Herrmann made of Cohen's work on ethics in 1907. Herrmann reminded Cohen of the fact that the more mature a man becomes religiously, the more concrete his religious involvement becomes and the less he speaks in universal conceptual language.[14] Herrmann divided his critique of Cohen's *Ethik des reinen Willens* (1904) into two reviews, and it is in the second, dealing with Cohen's attempt to find a place for religion within formal ethics, that Herrmann severely censures his failure. That Cohen was aware of this critique and its seriousness is attested to by his acknowledgment of them in his preface to

[11] Philosophical writings: *Schriften zur Philosophie und Zeitgeschichte*, 2 vols.; Jewish writings: *Juedische Schriften*, 3 vols.

[12] *Der Begriff der Religion im System der Philosophie* (Giessen, 1915).

[13] *Religion der Vernunft aus den Quellen des Judentums* (1919) (Frankfurt am Main, 1929).

[14] "Christliche Welt," March 7, 1907, pp. 222–28.

the second edition of the *Ethics* in 1907.[15] Cohen had entitled this ninth chapter of his book "Die Idee Gottes." In a struggle to avoid both pantheism and myth, the God that arose in this chapter could be defined only in the most abstract terminology. Cohen identified God and truth, and from this he deduced the ultimate harmony between nature and ethics. God as the source of truth is the guarantor that the world will be and that the moral law will be realized in it. This is about as much as ethics will allow to religion.

For Herrmann, religion is the discovery of the individual who is true to his longing for God.[16] Religion is not concerned with the world nor with past or future, but it is centered in the self and its own truth. The Protestantism of Herrmann is clear to the reader of Protestant thought from Luther to Schleiermacher. If the God of ethics is not adequate for religion, although it may be sufficient for the practical reason as an idea, then religion is grounded differently than ethics. It is rooted in a specific history and experience, it has a tradition, doctrines, dogmas, holy books, and ceremonies. We can speak of a religious life only with a shared heritage of values, a vision of the future, a redemptive history. Cohen brought Judaism into his philosophical system in his final two books; the consequences for his ethics is the subject of this study. The genesis of this study is Kant's *Metaphysics of Morals*, the Doctrine of Virtue, from which we proceed to a similar discussion in Cohen's *Ethics of the Pure Will* and finally to his doctrine of virtue in his *Religion of Reason*. If there has been a fundamental change in Cohen's thought, this can be detailed only in a comparative study of texts.

Kant published the *Metaphysics of Morals* in 1797, the second part of which is the *Tugendlehre* or the *Doctrine of Virtue*.[17] Kant had already declared that the realization of the moral law depended upon

[15] *Ethik*, XIII. "Ich habe mich bemueht, seinen Einwendungen nachzudenken, und ich habe an mehreren Stellen es versucht, ueber seinen Begriff der Religion mich mit ihm auseinanderzusetzen."

[16] "Christliche Welt," p. 224. "Nun, dieses Verlangen, in der Stille des eigenen Selbst wahrhaftig sein zu koennen, ist das Verlangen nach Gott." Ibid., p. 223. "In der Religion handelt es sich nie um die Welt, weder noch um das Weltganze noch um Ein zelnes in der Vergangenheit oder Zukunft, sodern allein um die innere Lebendigkeit des einzelnen Menschen."

[17] Immanuel Kant, *Metaphysik der Sitten*, ed. K. Vorlaender (Hamburg: Meiner Verlag, 1959). The two parts are: (1) *Metaphysische Anfangsgruende der Rechtslehre*, (2) *Metaphysiche Anfangsgruende der Tugendlehre*. English trans. of (1) *Metaphysical Elements of Justice*, trans. John Ladd (Indianapolis: Little Library of Liberal Arts, 1965), henceforth referred to as Ladd, and (2) *Metaphysical Principles of Virtue* (Indianapolis: Little Library of Liberal Arts, 1964), *The Doctrine of Virtue*, trans. Mary S. Gregor (Harper Torchbook, 1964), henceforth cited as Gregor.

the trust that man placed in it.[18] The moral strength, the will to manifest this trust as duty, is virtue. The concept of duty imposed upon us by the moral law necessitates us to adopt ends which are also duties. Virtue is the identity of duty and end. Moral human behavior in its sublime moments is virtue. The power to dominate the sensuous barriers raised against the pure practical reason links the sublime with moral feeling. The strength of virtue is the sublime example of man's trust in his moral purpose.

The metaphysical first principle of a doctrine of virtue must proceed from the form of the law avoiding all attempts to determine duties from either will, end, or feeling.[19] Man finds the idea of duty in his reason, for through reason alone do we discover that the essence of a thing is given in its form (*forma dat esse rei*).[20] The real danger for Kant is that a doctrine of virtue, if not based upon a moral concept of freedom, finally becomes eudaemonism. Although it is beyond the theoretical reason to know, it is necessary for the practical reason to suppose the moral idea of freedom whose reality can be given in experience. If the moral idea of freedom cannot be advanced by theoretical reason as knowable and thus transcendent, it can be advanced by the practical reason as thinkable and believable. The moral attitude of reason toward that which is stated as unknowable by theoretical reason is faith.[21] In the moral faith the moral world is constructed. Virtue is our ability to proceed with those moral maxims which the idea of a moral world demands.

A man can compel another to perform an action, he cannot compel him to have an end (*Zweck*). Kant, therefore, defines ethics "as the system of the ends of pure practical reason."[22] It is apparent that the ends which we ought to adopt are those dictated by pure practical reason. They raise the question, for what purpose should men have existed? (*Wozu haben Menschen existieren muessen?*) (*K.d.U.*, 339n). The realization of the moral law in man, the subject of morality, is the supreme purpose of creation. Although the idea of man as the subject of morality is believable and thinkable, its achievement necessitates a doctrine of duties and ends from which the moral education of mankind can be made intelligible.

18 Kant, *Kritik der Urteilskraft* (Leipzig: Meiner Verlag, 1948), p. 462 with note. "Es ist ein Vertrauen auf die Verheissung des moralischen Gesetzes; aber nicht als eine solche, die in demselben enthalten ist, sondern die ich hineinlege, und zwar aus moralisch hinreichendem Grunde."

19 *M.d.S.*, p. 377.

20 Immanuel Kant, *Von einem Neuerdings Erhobenen Vornehmen Ton in der Philosophie* (1796), in *Werke*, ed. Weischedel, III (Wiesbaden, 1958), 421. An important defense by Kant of his philosophic method against so-called philosophies of feeling.

21 *K.d.U.*, p. 402.

22 Gregor, p. 39; *M.d.S.*, p. 381. "Aus diesem Grunde kann die Ethik auch als das System der Zwecke der reinen praktischen Vernunft definiert sein."

Kant was well aware that man could never be certain of the moral purity of his purpose, and that if he sought to ground the maxim of his action in sensuous inclination and not in law he would destroy the possibility that his maxim could become universal law, i.e., a categorical imperative.[23] To put it differently, the cultivation of morality depends upon our ability to act out of duty from the pure motive of duty. In this sense, "virtue is self-constraint according to a principle of inner freedom, and so by the mere thought of one's duty in accordance with its formal law."[24] But virtue is more than self-contraint; it is man's power to promote ends which our moral reason puts forth. We become aware of our moral purpose through moral feeling which is awakened in us by actions in which the purposes of the practical reason are upheld over against the hindrances of sensibility. This feeling can be called sublime or even beautiful because it arises from an idea of man who is superior both to the nature within him and nature outside him. Although this feeling is the effect of the moral law within us, it is "the source of our awareness of the sublimity of this law and our moral purpose." Virtue is an ideal toward which there can only be an approximation, and every attempt to gain control of our inclination clarifies for us the dangers that threaten our conviction to promote the law of virtue.[25] We must not believe that we arbitrarily decide to promote or not promote this ideal of virtue. The ideal of virtue embodies the ought or the should be; we must deduce from this pure form maxims of behavior. These remarks are clarified with a clear summary from Kant's "Introduction" to the *Metaphysical Elements of Justice*:

> The [instructions of morality] command everyone without regard to his inclinations, solely because and insofar as he is free and has practical reason. Instruction in the laws of morality is not drawn from observation of oneself and the animality within him, nor from the perceptions of the world as to how things happen and how men in fact do act. But reason commands how one ought to act, even though no instance of such action can be found.[26]

[23] *M.d.S.*, pp. 392–93.

[24] *M.d.S.*, p. 394. " . . . so ist die Tugend . . . ein Zwang nach einem Prinzip der inneren Freiheit, mithin durch die blosse Vorstellung seiner Pflicht nach dem formalen Gesetz derselben." Gregor, p. 54.

[25] Gerhard Krueger, *Philosophie und Moral in der Kantischen Kritik* (1931) (Tuebingen, 1967), pp. 125–28.

[26] Ladd, pp. 15–16, *M.d.S.*: "Allein mit den Lehren der Sittlichkeit ist es anders bewandt. Sie gebieten fuer jedermann, ohne Ruecksicht auf seine Neigungen zu nehman bloss, weil und sofern er frei ist und praktische Vernunft hat. Die Belehrung in ihren Gesetzen ist nicht aus der Beobachtung seiner selbst und der Freiheit in ihm, nicht aus der Wahrnehmung des Weltlaufs geschoepft von dem, was geschieht und wie gehandelt wird, sondern die Vernunft gebietet, wie gehandelt werden soll, wenngleich noch kein Beispiel davon angetroffen wuerde. . . ."

The doctrine of virtue is intimately linked with Kant's differentiation between *sui iuris* and *sui dominus*.[27] If man is free and has practical reason, then he is a *simulacum divinitatis*. He cannot possess himself like a piece of external property to be arbitrarily used, *sui dominus*, but he is rightfully a possessor in his person, of humanity to which he has obligation, *sui iuris*. It is this humanity in his person that necessitates him to act as if he were the source of universal legislation. If he had this *ius disponendi de re sua*, the moral law would not command; he would not be the subject of morality, but the object of sensuous inclination. Man is a moral person because he can be obligated by the moral law.

The details of the doctrine begin with the division between negative and positive duties. Kant says:

> The negative duties forbid man to act contrary to the end of his nature, and so have to do merely with his moral self-preservation; the positive duties, which command him to make a certain object of choice his end, concern his perfecting of himself.[28]

From this distinction which we have previously made between *sui iuris and sui dominus* Kant rejects our right to *Selbstmord* or suicide. Man is the subject of morality, the agent of the moral law, the carrier of humanity. To arbitrarily destroy or mutilate his physical person is to do violence not only to natural life (*homo phaenomenon*) but to the moral law in us (*homo noumenon*). In an analogous way, suicide is a betrayal of obligation "if we think of man as leaving the post assigned to him in the world without having been called away."[29]

In the enumeration of negative and positive duties, the lie is given particular attention. Nothing threatens the moral subject more acutely than lying. The lie makes a man "contemptible" not only to his fellow man, but he becomes an object of contempt, *Verachtung*, to himself; he "annihilates his dignity as a man."[30] This corruption of moral substance can be viewed as a suffocation of man's noumenal reality, the death of moral freedom. In this death, violence arises, man has less worth than if he were a thing, *hat einen noch geringeren Wert, als wenn er bloss*

[27] *M.d.S*, p. 270.

[28] Gregor, p. 82, *M.d.S.*, p. 419: " . . . jene [negative duties] welche dem menschen in Ansehung des Zweckes seiner Natur verbieten, demselben zuwider zu handeln, mithin bloss auf die moralische Selbsterhaltung, diese [positive duties] welche gebieten, sich, einen gewissen Gegenstand der Willkuer zum Zweck zu machen, und auf die Vervollkommung seiner selbst gehen."

[29] Gregor, p. 85, *M.d.S.*, p. 422: "Diese [suicide] kann nun zwar auch als Uebertretung seiner Pflicht gegen andere Menschen . . . endlich auch gegen Gott, dessen uns anvertrauten Posten in der Welt der Menschen verlaesst, ohne davon abgerufen zu sein betrachtet werden."

[30] Gregor, p. 93, *M.d.S.*, p. 429: "Die Luege ist Wegwerfung und gleichsam Vernichtung seiner Menschenwuerde."

Sache waere.[31] He is thus usable, expendable, and one with whom communication is no longer possible. The lie induces moral chaos.

If in logic the possibility of a coherent discourse depends upon the principle of noncontradiction, in ethics the possibility of the same discourse would depend upon truthfulness, *Wahrhaftigkeit*. To speak philosophically is to attempt a meaningful discourse; the lie induces violence; the discourse is ended. In truthfulness the coherency begins again, meaning is revived, and man, as the moral subject, becomes again intelligible. To be truthful to himself is a command of the practical reason; the discourse between the noumenal and phaenomenal self, between the moral and natural being, is grounded in this truthfulness. Closely related to truthfulness is sincerity, the lack of which perpetuates deceitfulness, in terms of communication, a silence. Deeply incorporated in man's being is an inner judge, whom he can ignore, but if there is still the possibility of moral discourse we must assume he can still hear his voice.[32] Moral conscience, *Gewissen*, is the awareness of this inner voice which speaks the commands of the inner law. The law, expressed metaphorically, speaks; this speaking constitutes the moral substance of the noumenal. We can, however, discover no theoretical explanation of the causal relationship between the intelligible and the sensible; we must consider this causality, from the practical point of view, as a fact.[33]

If the idea of a Supreme Being can be posited at all, the theoretical reason, having denied all our supplications, causes us to turn to the practical reason and to analogy. We can view the Supreme Being as the Supreme Lawgiver, and we can hold the duties of virtue *as if* they were divine commands. This disposition of reason to believe in what is unattainable by theoretical cognition reveals a new realm of discourse whose source is in ideas, analogies, and moral faith.[34] It is upon this disposition

[31] *M.d.S.*, p. 429.

[32] *M.d.S.*, p. 438; "Jeder Mensch hat Gewissen und findet sich durch einen inneren Richter beobachtet; . . . Er kann sich zwar durch Lueste und Zerstreuungen betaeuben . . . aber nicht vermeiden, dann und wann zu sich selbst zu kommen oder zu erwachen, wo er alsbald die furchtbare Stimme desselben vernimmt . . . aber sie zu 'hoeren', kann er doch nicht vermeiden."

[33] *M.d.S.*, p. 439n.

[34] Gregor, pp. 105–6: ". . . to think of conscientiousness (which is also called religion) as responsibility before a holy Being (morally legislative reason) distinct from man yet present in his inmost being, and to submit himself to the will of this Being, as the rules of justice. Man's conception of religion as such is here only a 'principle of regarding all his duties *as if* they were divine Commandments.'" *M.d.S.*, p. 440: "Die Gewissenhaftigkeit (welche auch religio genannt wird) als Verantwortlichkeit vor einem von uns selbst unterschiedenen aber uns doch innigst gegenwaertigen heiligen Wesen (der moralischgesetzgebenen Vernunft) sich vorzustellen, und dessen Willen den Regeln der Gerechtigkeit zu unterwerfen. Der Begriff von der Religion ueberhaupt ist hier dem Menschen bloss 'ein Prinzip der Beurteilung aller seiner Pflichten als goettliche Gebote.'"

that the metaphysical principles of virtue are meaningfully explored.

We are concerned not only with what we can know, but with what we can think; not only with a constitutive principle for the determinant judgment, but with a regulative principle for the reflective judgment. Man needs the idea of God to understand his place in the universe and to grasp the fact that he is the subject of the moral law. God is the source of the truth of the moral law; the moral law is the ground of our awareness of God. In this awareness we become dutiful toward our moral destiny; the realization of humanity in ourselves and in relation to our fellow man. The final purpose of nature and of history becomes meaningful when they are understood as the necessary vehicles for the promotion of the moral law. We must thus conceive of God as that Supreme Being whose truth is the source of meaning for both nature and history. Our moral faith in God is our faith in the final moral victory of man. "In this [practical] sense it can therefore be said: to have religion is a duty of man to himself."[35]

Among other duties which man has to himself is the cultivation of the dispositions and powers which can enhance the development of his reason. If we think of ourselves as custodians of reason, as dwellings which only a holy law can inhabit, and in which it also finds its *causa cognoscendi*, this command to cultivate these dispositions becomes necessary. Kant puts it clearly: "it is a command of morally practical reason and a duty of man to cultivate his powers, and to be, from a pragmatic point of view, a man equal to the end of his existence."[36] It is the cultivation of the *Geisteskraefte*, the powers of the mind, which makes possible the world of rational and aesthetical ideas not limited by experience or guided by the rules of the understanding; it is the cultivation of our awareness not only of a world that is possibly *know*able, but is also *think*able. Man has duties to the *Seelenkraefte*, the powers of the soul, to our understanding (*Verstand*), similar to our powers of explication, memory, and imagination. There are also duties to our *Leibeskraefte*, powers of the body, because the health of the body is fundamental for

[35] Gregor, p. 110, *M.d.S.*, p. 444: "In diesem (praktischen) Sinn kann es also so lauten: Religion zu haben ist Pflicht des Menschen gegen sich selbst."

Important also is Kant's statement in the same paragraph: "For this idea [of God] proceeds entirely from our own reason and *we ourselves make it*." "Denn da diese Idee ganz aus unserer eigenen Vernunft hervorgeht and *von uns . . . selbst gemacht wird*." It is to be emphasized here that man is the source of his highest truth and that this truth depends upon him. In contradiction to the theoretical cognition whose source is experience, the practical reason has no such power source but must depend upon the cultivation of our reflective judgment.

[36] Gregor, p. 111, *M.d.S.*, p. 445: ". . . es ist Gebot der moralischpraktischen Vernunft und Pflicht des Menschen gegen sich selbst, Seine Vermoegen anzubauen und in pragmatischer Ruecksicht ein dem Zweck seines Daseins angemessener Mensch zu sein."

the realization of man's end.[37] If we are to decide which of these powers we should cultivate and to what degree, the importance of self-knowledge becomes clear. We choose on the basis of an evaluation of our capacities, but in all this lies the duty that man has to himself "to be a useful member of the world, since this also belongs to the worth of humanity in his own person, which he ought not degrade."[38]

The second part of the text introduces the realm of mutual relationship, which Kant divides between those duties which obligate man to man and those duties which are man's due and subsequently cause no obligation. Love belongs to the former and respect to the latter.[39] To clarify the word *love*, we must put aside any identification with feeling or emotion and say that love is "a maxim of benevolence (practical love)," *Maxime des Wohlwollens*. Respect is a maxim of self-esteem for the dignity of humanity in the other person, *die Wuerde der Menschheit in einer anderen Person*.[40]

Kant divides the duties of love into (1) beneficence, (2) gratitude, and (3) sympathy. "Beneficence is the maxim of making another's happiness one's end."[41] Reason necessitates the adoption of this maxim as a universal law. It is the dictorial legislative will of the practical reason which makes it possible for man to be ruler of both self-interest and nature. It is the belief in this will which rejects the cynicism of Hobbes, the theorist of commercial society, that all men act on the basis of self-interest. We cannot talk philosophically unless beneficence is a possibility and the categorical imperative does have legislative force. It would seem that when Kant introduces a universal duty such as beneficence, he is aware that the more natural disposition of man is self-interest, but the philosophic duty is to the *should be*. We can be resigned to what *is*; the *should be* is the problem.

The second duty of love is gratitude. "Gratitude consists in honoring a person because of a kindness he has done us."[42] But not only is gratitude a duty, it is a holy duty, *heilige Pflicht*. The obligation cannot be requited by a subsequent benevolence because there is a "priority of merit," *Vorzug des Verdienstes*. From an ethical position Kant proceeds to an historical

[37] Gregor, pp. 111–12, *M.d.S.*, p. 445, 446.

[38] Gregor, p. 112, *M.d.S.*, p. 446: ". . . es ist Pflicht des Menschen gegen sich selbst, ein der Welt nuetzliches Glied zu sein, weil dieses auch zum Wert der Menschheit in seiner eigenen Person gehoert, die er also nicht abwuerdigen soll."

[39] *M.d.S.*, p. 449: "Vermoege des Prinzips der Wechselliebe sind sie angewiesen, sich einander bestaendig zu naehern; durch das der *Achtung*, die sie einander schuldig sind, sich im Abstande von einander zu erhalten. . . ."

[40] *M.d.S.*, p. 449.

[41] Gregor, p. 120, *M.d.S.*, p. 452: "Wohltun aber die Maxime, sich dasselbe (dem Wohlsein anderer) zum Zweck zu machen. . . ."

[42] Gregor, p. 123, *M.d.S.*, p. 455: "Dankbarkeit ist die Verehrung einer Person wegen einer uns erwiesenen Wohltat."

one. Gratitude is extended through the ages, and although we do not necessarily evaluate the past more highly than the present, there is the contribution of age to age and the gratitude of one to the other is the ground of all further achievement and development. It is difficult to think of a present or a future without a past, and the philosophic discourse implies in its coherency a discourse across the periodizations of time. In it there is developed a sensitivity to the contributions of others and an appreciation for the mutuality effort which belongs to human progress.

"Sympathetic joy and sorrow are really sensuous feelings of a pleasure or pain at another's state of happiness or sadness."[43] Kant maintains that nature has endowed us with a susceptibility (*Empfaenglichkeit*) to feel pleasure and pain with others (*humanitas aesthetica*). In the second and third sections of the Introduction to the *Critique of Judgment* Kant had defined the aesthetic facility as standing between the faculty of theoretical knowledge and the autonomy of practical reason. The aesthetic faculty thus stands closest to man; it is the most subjective, adds nothing to the object but, in relation to it, is the feeling of pleasure or pain. Since the aesthetic judgment does not proceed according to concepts, but in respect to objects of nature, the cultivation of this feeling depends upon the sensuous and man must seek the poor, the prisoner, the sick. If we seek to avoid these situations because of the painful feelings which they arouse, the thought of duty is all that remains, the mere "will to share" (*humanitas practica*).[44] Here we learn how to convert that respect for humanity in our own person into respect for the object.[45] The sympathetic feeling of pain evoked by the suffering of others indicates that nature has implanted in us impulses and feelings whose cultivation and education are necessary moral duties. We are not abandoned to the efficacy of the moral law, opposed and deserted by our impulses and feelings. Their education and articulation in concrete situations of human ill and misfortune bring forth the possibility of similar design in the natural and rational aspect of man.[46] Kant's pedagogical schemes reflect his conviction that the impulses and feelings do not have to be suppressed, but can be transformed into meaningful expressions of moral obligation. It is

[43] Gregor, p. 125, *M.d.S.*, p. 456: "Mitfreude und Mitleid sind zwar sinnliche Gefuehle einer Lust oder Unlust an dem Zustande des Vergnuegens sowohl als Schmerzens anderer. . . ."

[44] Gregor, p. 125.

[45] *K.d.U.*, p. 97, par. 27: "Verwechslung einer Achtung fuer das Objekt, statt der fuer die Idee der Menschheit in unserem Subjekte."

[46] *M.d.S.*, p. 457, par. 35. This paragraph is important because it shows the concrete aspect of the Kantian ethic, if one wants to see it. "So ist es Pflicht nicht die Stellen, wo sich Arme befinden, denen das Notwendigste abgeht, zu umgehen sondern sie aufzusuchen, nicht die Krankenstuben oder die Gefaengnisse der Schuldner und dergl. zu fliehen. . . ."

in this sense that the alleviation of suffering belongs not only to the impulse or feeling, but to the idea of humanity; not only to the situation of moment, but to the future history of man. Education cultivates the "seeds of the good," *Keime zum Guten*, into the idea of the "universal good," *Weltbeste*.[47]

Similar to the duties of love, Kant enumerates duties of respect to other men. There is a duty to acknowledge the dignity of humanity in our fellow man. We can illuminate this duty more fully if we affirm that the self-respect which a man has for himself and his reason should not be disdained by our behavior or attitude.[48] The worth or dignity of humanity in man is not an exchangeable commodity which can be given an exchange value; we have here a noumenal person, the source of legislative reason. To disdain this noumenal person and to hold it worthless is to destroy the barrier against all those vices, envy, ingratitude, and malicious joy which Kant holds to be contrary to the love of man.[49] The violation of the duty of respect, the lack of esteem for the humanity of our fellow man, terminates that ethical intercourse upon which all progress toward the idea of the Good depends. The ground of that intercourse is: "Every man has a rightful claim to respect from his fellow man and is reciprocally obligated to show respect for every other man."[50]

Experience can never provide an object that can adequately correspond to an idea. The gap appears to be unredeemable and yet desirable. If the idea can never be realized as an object of experience, perfection is excluded from the world of time and space. In this world of appearance there is only approximation. The contrast between appearance and the *Ding an sich* is permanent, allowing to the object of experience the possibilities of cognition denied to the perfection of the idea as the *Ding an sich*. Here we speak of the idea as a "principle of comprehension" that must be distinguished carefully from the concept, the "condition of explication." Since the ideas are regulative and not constitutive, thinkable but not knowable, they explicate the *should be* of experience but do not constitute it. Ideas are always contingent to experience. Friendship and the perfect juridical constitution exemplify the idea as a reflective possibility and at the same time an object of moral faith.

"Friendship (considered in its perfection) is the union of two persons

[47] Immanuel Kant, *Ueber Paedagogik* (1803), ed. F. T. Rink, in Kant, *Werke*, ed. W. Weischedel, VI, 704–5; English ed., *Education* (Ann Arbor, 1964).

[48] Gregor, p. 133, *M.d.S.*, p. 463n.

[49] Gregor, pp. 127–30, a general discussion of these vices.

[50] Gregor, p. 132, *M.d.S.*, p. 462: "Ein jeder Mensch hat rechtmaessigen Anspruch auf Achtung von sinen Nebenmenschen, und wechselseitig ist er dazu auch gegen jeden anderen verbunden."

through equal and mutual love and respect."[51] There is duty of reason which commands us to strive for such friendship, the mutual concern of men for each other, the advancement of their welfare, their moral good. But the idea of friendship "is a mere idea," *eine blosse Idee*, although a practically necessary one, *aber doch praktisch notwendig*.[52] We cannot know what essentially is the welfare of the other, and we can never be sure of our impulses. Can we be sure that we are acting from the duty of friendship? Yet friendship is a duty, a "duty of honor," *ehrenvolle Pflicht*. The difficulties in the way of the achievement of this duty appear insurmountable if only from the interplay of love and respect. We can observe the demands of one countermanded by those of the other.[53] Friendship is so delicate a relationship that it cannot be allowed to rest on feelings or be exposed to excessive familiarity. Respect limits this familiarity; to treat the friend as an end and not as a means is to be conscious of his separate existence, distinct in needs and talents.

"Moral friendship is the complete confidence of two persons in revealing their secret thoughts and feelings to each other, in so far as such disclosures are consistent with mutual respect for each other."[54] The fear of being used by others or their lack of discretion are the barriers to this moral friendship. If the moral friendship is rare, is not the pragmatic friendship perhaps nonexistent? This latter type of friendship assumes that we can make the ends of others our own. Even though the motive might be love, the purity necessary for a maxim is absent. Kant believed that the moral friendship existed, but that pragmatic friendship "is an ideal of our wishes, which knows no bounds in the concept of pure reason but which must always be very limited in experience."[55] Friendships, like peace, are the ideals we project, and, although painfully aware of their absence, we are necessitated to strive for them as duties of reason. We cannot disdain of our efforts because the idea can never be fully realized. In fact, the reverse might be true: our efforts impelled by reason lead to a heightened esteem of our moral worth. "It is, moreover, only by acknowledging and complying with imperatives that we can

[51] Gregor, p. 140, *M.d.S.*, p. 469: "Freundschaft (in ihrer Vollkommenheit betrachtet) ist die Vereinigung zweier Personen durch gleiche wechselseitige Liebe und Achtung."

[52] Gregor, p. 140.

[53] Gregor, p. 142. Kant seems pressed to give examples and explanations of the delicacies of the friendship relationship. Perhaps no other human relationship makes us so aware of our inadequacies than this duty of friendship, and how rare is the friend and virtuous man.

[54] Gregor, p. 143, *M.d.S.*, p. 471: "Moralische Freundschaft ist das voellige Vertrauen zweier Personen in wechselseitiger Eroeffnung ihrer geheimen Urteile und Empfindungen, soweit sie mit beiderseitiger Achtung gegen einander bestehen kann."

[55] Gregor, p. 143, *M.d.S.*, p. 472: ". . . ist ein Ideal des Wunsches, das im Vernunftbegriff keine Grenzen kennt, in der Erfahrung aber doch immer sehr begrenzt werden muss."

maintain the very distinction between the factual and valuational and are able to decide in favor of the latter."[56]

The *Critique of Practical Reason* Kant divides into the *Doctrine of the Elements of the Pure Practical Reason* and the *Methodology of the Pure Practical Reason*. Methodology implies "the way in which we can secure to the laws of pure practical reason access to the human mind and an influence on its maxims. That is to say, it is the way we can make the objectively practical reason also subjectively practical."[57] In a similar fashion the *Ethical Doctrine of Method, Ethische Methodenlehre*, explores the means by which the pure practical reason is able to control the inclinations. Virtue is the consequence of this struggle; it is not the result of a resolve, but the actualization of it through strength, discipline, and courage. There is no direct route from willing to doing, "for one *cannot* straightway do all that one *wills* to do."[58] If we must find ways of making the pure practical reason subjectively practical, we cannot logically be limited in our search by the determinant judgment, but logic "should also provide rules for preparatory judgments," *vorlaeufige Urteile*,[59] by which new thoughts, *Gedanken*, become possible. These preparatory judgments are inventive projections of the imagination for which concepts have not yet been found but are sought. The problem becomes one of seeking concepts for a sensible reality whose elusiveness seems to defy conceptualization.[60] Kant exemplifies this problem: "The pupil, who thus sees that he is able to think for himself, provides, by his questions about obscurities or doubts in the propositions admitted, occasion for the teacher to learn how to question skillfully, according to the saying *docendo discimus*" (we learn by teaching).[61] In reference to

[56] N. Rotenstreich, *Spirit and Man* (The Hague, 1963), pp. 251–52.

[57] Immanuel Kant, *Critique of Practical Reason*, trans. L. W. Beck (Chicago, 1949), p. 249. *Kritik der praktischen Vernunft*, ed. Karl Vorlaender (Leipzig, 1949), p. 269: "Vielmehr wird unter dieser Methodenlehre die Art verstanden, wie man den Gesetzen der reinen praktischen Vernunft Eingang in das menschliche Gemuet, Einfluss auf die Maximen desselben verschaffen, d.i. die objektiv praktische Vernunft auch subjektiv praktisch machen koenne."

[58] Gregor, p. 149, *M.d.S.*, p. 477: ". . . denn man *kann* nicht alles sofort, was man *will*. . . ."

[59] Ibid., p. 150.

[60] E. Weil, *Problèmes Kantiens* (Paris, 1963), p. 64: "La judiciaire [as analyzed in the *Critique of Judgment*] assume ainsi une nouvelle tâche. Jusqu'ici, la seule fonction avait été de subsumer le donné sous les concepts, soit fondamentaux, soit construits à partir de l'expérience; le nouveau problème fait qu'elle change de direction dans son travail et que, au bien de classer le donné sensible sous le donné théorique, elle se mette à chercher le concept sous lequel elle pourrait placer ce qu'elle recontre. Elle cesse d'être *déterminante* et se fait réfléchissante."

[61] Gregor, p. 150, *M.d.S.*, p. 478: "Der Lehrling, welcher hierbei inne wird, dass er selbst zu denken vermoege, veranlasst durch seine Gegenfragen (ueber Dunkelheit oder den eingeraeumten Saetzen entgegenstehende Zweifel), dass der Lehrer noch dem docendo discimus selbst lernt."

education, Kant remarks that the teacher should not use the model child to deduce conduct for all the others; the consequence could only be that this model child would be disliked. Education is an art; "the subjective autonomy of each man's practical reason" cannot be developed and disciplined through mechanistic imitation of others but must be discovered and explored for itself. Education involves experimentation, and it is important to note that Kant was in favor of experimental schools. This is significant because it links so intimately theory and practice. Kant says: "People imagine, indeed, that experiments in education are unnecessary, and that we can judge from our reason whether anything is good or not. This is a great mistake, and experience teaches us that the results of an experiment are often entirely different from what we expected."[62]

Kant developed a moral catechism to demonstrate the efficacy of the dialogic method. The conversation between teacher and pupil concerns the question of happiness, but on a deeper level the real problem is that of the worthiness to be happy. Through question and answer it is possible to make the pupil aware that the worthiness follows from reason, and the desire for sheer happiness from inclination. Inventiveness, experimentation, skill on the part of the teacher can make it possible for the pupil to reach the conclusion "that if we do not make ourselves *unworthy of happiness* by violating our duty, we can also hope to *share* in happiness."[63] Of great importance for the question of method is Kant's statement, "the greatest care must be taken *not* to base the command of duty on the fact that it is actually observed by the men it is supposed to obligate, nor even on the advantage or detriment to others flowing from it."[64] The model examples of others can in no way induce us to take the moral principle seriously. The principle does not obtain its worth because others have acted in accordance with it; its worth must be discovered by each man anew. If the concept of duty or the sublimity of virtue is to be sacrificed to inclination, feeling, or passion, the consequences must be weighed and it is these contemplated consequences rather than the lapidary example of others that make the moral dialogue possible and meaningful. The dialogue is thus possible when there are

[62] *Education*, p. 22, *Ueber Paedagogik*, p. 708: "Man bildet sich zwar insgemein ein, dass Experimente bei der Erziehung nicht noetig waeren, und dass mann shon aus der Vernunft urteilen koenne, ob etwas gut, oder nicht gut sein werde. Man irret hierin aber sehr, und die Erfahrung lehrt, dass sich oft bei unseren Versuchen ganz entgegengesetzte Wirkungen zeigen von denen, die man erwartete."

[63] Gregor, p. 156, *M.d.S.*, p. 482: ". . . wenn wir uns nicht selbst der Gluechseligkeit unwuerdig machen, welche durch Uebertretung unserer Pflicht geschieht, wir hoffen koennen, ihrer teilhaftig zu werden."

[64] Gregor, p. 156, *M.d.S.*, p. 482: ". . . ist die groesste Aufmerksamkeit darauf zu richten, dass das Pflichtgebot ja *nicht* auf die aus dessen Beobachtung fuer den Menschen, den es verbinden soll, ja selbst auch nicht einmal fuer andere fliessenden Vorteile oder Nachteile. . . ."

viable alternatives: the moral principle, pragmatic precepts, or utilitarianism. The dialogue must be extended to encompass casuistical questions because "by this sort of practice, the pupil is drawn unwittingly to an *interest* in morality."[65] The search for methodology is the exploration of the reflective and preparatory judgment. In this respect Kant warns against allowing the religious catechism to precede the moral catechism because this would force the pupil to "embrace duties out of fear and feign interest in them which is not in his heart."[66]

The last sections of the doctrine of method deal with religion, and this is proper to a philosophical morality only if religion is defined as: "the sum of all duties *as if* they were divine commands."[67] The idea of God is the construct of reason; we do not speak of a Being apart from our idea of Him. Moral theology requires "a determinate concept of the Supreme Cause of the world according to moral laws and, consequently, to the concept of such a cause as satisfies our moral final purpose."[68] If we avoid the moral teleology, the idea of a Supreme Cause, is not the moral destiny of man and creation, at the same time, voided? If man is not the *causa cognoscendi* of God, the duties which man has to himself become pragmatic precepts; that God creates himself in man's reason, in the moral imperatives, forces the conclusion that in the legislative expression of the moral law the Supreme Being is created.[69] This moral faith in God is analogous to a moral faith in the idea of humanity; the duty in regard to God is the duty to ourselves; our faith in Him is morally commanding us. "It [duty to God] is not an objective obligation to fulfill certain services to another person, but only a subjective obligation to strengthen the moral motive in our own legislative reason."[70] God for Kant is presupposed by reason as idea; the God of revealed religion *exists*, and the very fact that he *exists* and is experienced excludes such religious reality from all pure philosophical morality. The prophet and

[65] Gregor, p. 158, *M.d.S.*, p. 484: ". . . und so der Lehrling durch dergleichen Uebung unvermerkt in das Interesse der Sittlichkeit gezogen wird."

[66] Gregor, p. 158, *M.d.S.*, p. 484: ". . . sich aus Furcht zu pflichten zu bekennen und eine Teilnahme an derselben, die nicht im Herzen ist, zu luegen."

[67] Gregor, p. 162, *M.d.S.*, p. 487: ". . . der Inbegriff aller Pflichten als goettliche Gebote."

[68] *K.d.U.*, par. 91: ". . . naemlich auf einem bestimmten Begriff der Obersten Ursache als Weltursache nach moralischen Gesetzen, mithin einer solchen, die unserem moralischen Endzwecke Genuege tut . . ." (English trans. of J. H. Bernard, p. 334). This whole section should be read for an understanding of the significance of the teleological judgment.

[69] Rotenstreich, p. 251. "Thus the notion of the imperative as expressed concretely in the demand that man's position as a subject be acknowledged and maintained per se is both the pre-condition and an essential material component of the ethical domain."

[70] Gregor, p. 162, *M.d.S.*, p. 487: ". . . nicht objektive, die Verbindlichkeit zur Leistung gewisser Dienste an einen anderen, sondern nur subjektive, zur Staerkung der moralischen Triebfeder in unserer eigenen gesetzgebenden Vernunft."

the philosopher have no dialogue. Tradition, doctrine, dogmas, rites and customs, etc.—basic ingredients of revealed religion—do not complete ethics; in fact, ethics passionately loyal to the autonomy of the pure practical reason could only find its purity violated by these ingredients.

Ethics are fundamentally involved in the reciprocal duties among men in terms of love and respect. If we speak of the relations between man and God, the terms of love and respect become less understandable. God, we must assume, has only rights and no duties, and toward Him man would thus have duties and no rights. If these assumptions are maintained, then we must conclude that the relationship between God and man has as its basis a transcendent principle. Ethics affirm that "the moral relation of men to men, whose will reciprocally limits one another, has an immanent principle."[71] Since we can ascribe to God nothing cognizable, we can speak neither in terms of his understanding nor his justice, love, or beneficence. What we have is moral faith, "a trust in the promise of the moral law, not however such as is contained in it, but such as I put into it and that on morally adequate grounds."[72] The realization of the moral law, therefore, depends upon man and the trust which he places in it. This trust must come freely from him and not through tradition or dogma; there can be no feeling of having been bound by external factors. Kant puts it precisely: "It is a free belief, not in that for which dogmatical proofs for the theoretically determinant judgment are to be found or in that to which we hold ourselves bound, but in that which we assume on behalf of a design in accordance with the laws of freedom."[73] Freedom is our capacity to extend reason beyond the limits to which the theoretical concept is restricted. It is in freedom that the rational ideas have their genesis, and although they lack a theoretical ground of validity, the efficacy of their reality is our trust, *Vertrauen*. The idea of a public law of nations, the idea of perpetual peace, the idea of a world community of states, are examples of the trust of men who stand in relations to principles which are unconditioned.

Virtue implies the command to self-mastery, and although it is an ideal which is perhaps unattainable, the duty of virtue remains a command. We are not limited to what can be known; through the pure practical reason we are aware of a morally legislative reason, and through a

[71] Gregor, p. 104, *M.d.S.*, p. 488: ". . . dagegen [over against the relation of God to man] das der Menschen gegen Menschen deren Wille gegeneinander wechselseitig einschraenkend ist, ein immanentes Prinzip hat."

[72] *K.d.U.*, p. 462n: "Es ist ein Vertrauen auf die Verheissung des moralischen Gesetzes; aber nicht als eine solche, die in demselben enthalten ist, sondern die ich hineinlege, und zwar aus moralisch hinreichendem Grunde."

[73] *K.d.U.*, p. 463 (Bernard, p. 324): "Es ist ein freies Fuerwahrhalten nicht dessen, wozu dogmatische Beweise fuer die theoretisch bestimmende Urteilskraft anzutreffen sind, noch wozu wir uns verbunden halten, sondern dessen, war wir zum Behuf einer Absicht noch Gesetzen der Freiheit annehmen. . . ."

moral teleology we realize that ideas can be assumed and assented to and that true moral faith "is trust in the attainment of a design, the promotion of which is a duty, but the possibility of the fulfillment of which is not to be comprehended by us."[74]

[74] *K.d.U.*, p. 463: "Der Glaube ist ein Vertrauen zu der Erreichung einer Absicht, deren Befoerderung Pflicht, die Moeglichkeit der Ausfuehrung derselben aber fuer uns nicht *einzusehen* ist."

See also Rotenstreich, p. 231: "While our capacity to realize the good doubtlessly involves a factual power, it also involves a power to leap, so to speak, beyond the level of fact and to dwell at the level of values."

Chapter II

HERMANN COHEN'S DOCTRINE OF VIRTUES

Hermann Cohen devoted two works to the specific problem of ethics. In 1877 he wrote an interpretive study of Kant's ethics, *Kants Begruendung der Ethik*, and finally in 1904 as part of his own philosophical system he wrote the *Ethic des reinen Willens*. It is in this latter book that Cohen deals with the concept of virtue (2d edition, 1907; all references are to this edition). Kant defined virtue as a moral strength whose significance becomes apparent when we face the problem of how to comply with a legislative reason, i.e., the categorical imperative, in the concrete situation. Kant attempted to avoid dogmatic answers to this problem; he was deeply aware that concrete man was far from being susceptible to the demands of the categorical imperative and ways had to be found through experience which would make it possible, if it were at all possible, to go from the categorical imperative to right action in the concrete situation.[1]

Cohen begins the discussion of virtue by stating that duty, *Pflicht*, is the content of obligation, *Verbindlichkeit*, implied in the moral law. It is through duty that the imperative of the moral law is actualized.[2] Virtue is a disposition, *Gesinnung*, to act out of duty. It is a moral strength that is cultivated and educated by the moral deed. It is not only our awareness of our obligation to act that constitutes virtue, but that assurance that we will act because we have acted before.[3] This self-mastery is the vital source of virtue. It is the categorical imperative which commands what we should do; that we can do it depends upon what we have done and the development of our disposition to act out of obligation. Virtue is a measure of our ability to act from duty for the sake of duty. The realization of this possibility reflects an inner harmony between the disposition to act and the act

[1] See Kant's important work *Anthropologie in pragmatischer Hinsicht*, in *Werke*, ed. Weischedel, 6th ed. (Frankfurt am Main, 1964).

[2] *Ethik*, p. 472: ". . . dass der Pflicht dagegen nur fuer die Anwendung des Sittengesetzes auf den Menschen der Raum eroeffnet ward. Die Pflicht wird so zum Grundbegriffe der angewandten Ethik."

[3] *Ethik*, p. 476: ". . . aber um diesen Weg [of duty] mit sicherheit, mit Stetigkeit zu verfolgen, so dass die Selbstbestimmung nicht bei jedem Schritte ein harter Kampf werden muss; sondern wie aus dem Grunde der Selbsterhaltung sich ergeben kann."

itself. Cohen stresses the constancy of act as the creative source of virtue; it is not possible to speak of virtue unless we speak of persistency, *Bestaendigkeit.*

Virtue is a path to moral self-consciousness.[4] All the virtues lead to the same goal, to this self-consciousness. The affect of this self-consciousness is honor, *Ehre*, a term that he prefers to respect, *Achtung*, or dignity, *Wuerde*. Honor implies a firm and more empirical sense of equality. It can be compared to the coin whose value is equal in every hand. Honor is reflected in a similar way in the face of each man. The word must have a concreteness which defies the possibility of a vague determination. Honor for Cohen has the preciseness of juridical or mathematical clarity. To avoid any hint of relativity and to stress totality necessitates Cohen's desire to give to honor this exact and precise value.[5] Each man bears in him honor, which means that we honor this essence which is constitutive of him. In this all men are equal; the moral self-consciousness is the expression of this total equality of men. Virtue, the path to self-consciousness, is the specific realization of the equality of man. This must be extended to political life and international relations. Ultimately, the articulation of the equality passes from the dimensions of individual relations to political and then to international; the totality of the concept would imply these degrees of extension.

Love proceeds from the *I*, but honor must be derived from the *You*, which in turn is the source of the *We*.[6] We honor the subject of morality in each man. The equality of this subject in all men gives rise to the concept of totality. In each *You* inhabits totality. Virtue is the strength of will which allows us to follow the path to moral self-consciousness. The affect of each approximation to virtue is honor,[7] the awareness that we are involved in the problem of virtue. This ethical problem precedes our acceptance or rejection of its demands. We are *a priori* seized by the demand of virtue and its affect in honor. It is alive both in our denial and our affirmation.

The affect of honor is a feeling of honor, *Ehrgefuehl*, a feeling which is born in the equality of man. This equality is a moral one, rooted in the moral faith that virtue is a possibility, that moral self-consciousness is a

[4] Cohen speaks of virtue as a signpost, *Wegweiser*. *Ethik*, p. 478: ". . . die Tugend soll einem Wegweiser bilden, der auf geradem Wege zu jenem Ziel [moral self-consciousness] sicher hinfuehrt."

[5] *Ethik*, p. 495: "Die Ehre dagegen hat ihren Namen vom Muenzwert (aes). Sie wirkt mit der Unfehlbarkeit eines Naturzwangs; und dieser Zwang uebt kein konventionelle Macht, keine Scheingroesse der Erfahrung und der Einbildung; nicht einmal irgendein aesthetischem Reiz aus; sondern einzig und allein die menschliche Gestalt."

[6] *Ethik*, p. 497: "Denn wie die Liebe aus dem Ich quillt, so die Ehre aus dem Du. Und so kittet sie vermoege des Du das Wir."

[7] *Ethik*, p. 490. More precisely, Cohen says: "Die Ehre ist der Affekt der Tugend."

fact, that a moral legislative reason should be imposed upon inclination and sensuality. Honor is faith in a value that places the meaning of man in his moral substance. If this value is revealed in some men through virtue, honor holds the obligation to virtue as nevertheless binding in all men. In addition, it holds that the virtuous man is bound to his fellow man, whatever his cultural level, to act with virtue. This equality which honor necessitates is as much political as it is moral.[8]

Cohen begins his discussion of the virtues with truthfulness. Previously Kant had considered the virtue of truthfulness, *Wahrhaftigkeit*, as inseparable from a discussion of the lie. The lie brings contempt for the dignity of man; it does violence to the subject of morality and the moral discourse. There is a split that ends communication between the moral and natural being. Truthfulness for Cohen is the source of the moral self. This self is neither divinely given nor an inborn fact; its reality is the subject of the moral problem.[9] Truthfulness is a faith in knowledge as the source of truth. The object of truthfulness is knowledge; the path which it indicates is self-knowledge, self-consciousness.[10] Truthfulness and truth merge in thought; thus, the moral self that emerges in truthfulness is the true self, the self of truth. The self is the ground of truth; it is the subject of moral law. The self is totality; virtue is the achievement of the knowledge of this self in self-knowledge and self-consciousness. The problem of the self in its historical manifestations is the problem of thought which brings and returns every moment of diversity or multiplicity to totality. It is in this respect that Cohen says that virtue is knowledge and that self-knowledge stands under the demand of truthfulness which imposes constant self-evaluation.[11] Thus, if totality is the category of the moral self, all the virtues are guides and paths leading to totality through knowledge.

Every moment of life bears in it the obligation for self-exploration. This is demanded by truthfulness; each moment renews the obligation; each moment sets anew this task, *Aufgabe*.[12] The self emerges from that

[8] *Ethik*, p. 496: "Das Wesen des Menschen ist seine Ehre; seine Menschenehre. In dieser Menschenehre sind die Menschen gleich. Der Kulturmensch wird zum Barbar, wenn er den Wilden nicht als Menschen behandelt. Der Ehre ist die politische Nutzanwendung eingeboren."

[9] *Ethik*, p. 505: "Das Selbst ist nicht eine Seele, welche dir angeboren ist; es ist ueberhaupt keine Sache, kein Besitz: es ist ein Ausdruck des allgemeinen sittlichen Problems."

[10] *Ethik*, pp. 505–6: "Das Selbstbewusstsein ist Selbsterkenntnis. Diese bedeutet fuer die Tugend der Wahrhaftigkeit; nur in der Selbsterkenntnis besteht das Selbst."

[11] *Ethik*, p. 504: "Die Tugend ist Erkenntnis; die Erkenntnis aber hat zum vornehmsten Inhalte das Selbst." See also p. 505: "Die Wahrhaftigkeit fordert fuer die Selbsterkenntnis bestaendige Selbstpruefung und Selbstkontrolle. Dazu gehoert echtes Denken, welches verschieden ist von phantastischen Gruebein."

[12] *Ethik*, p. 507: "Kein Mensch darf an sich glauben, in keinem Momente seines Lebens. Seine Erkenntnis muss es ihm zur Einsicht bringen, wenn seine Sittlichkeit es nicht fordern

movement which is inherent in the relationship between being and its ground in the *should be*. Both moments of this relationship constitute the ethical problem, inseparable, constitutive moments of self-knowledge and self-consciousness. The virtue of truthfulness impels us to base moral education upon theoretical knowledge.[13] In this requirement of truthfulness, ethics is made independent of religion.[14]

The virtue of truthfulness belongs equally to theoretical as well as to practical knowledge. Science, *Wissenschaft*, and morality, *Sittlichkeit*, are rooted in the same fundamental law of truth, and it is in the virtue of truthfulness that the totality of science and morality is assumed both as fact and obligation.[15] The concern for science cannot be separated from the concern for morality. There is only one calling, and that is truth. The awareness and the responsibility to the singularity of this calling are virtue. If, as Cohen implies, virtue is knowledge, then virtue as truthfulness is what makes us aware and holds us responsible to the totality of knowledge as the fundamental law, *Grundgesetz*, of truth. Truthfulness is the virtue of philosophy.[16] It is the guide, *Wegweiser*, for science as well as ethics; it makes possible the coherent philosophical dialogue; and it is the barrier against the violence of thought which is introduced by the alleged division between ethics and science. The virtue of philosophy is the virtue of totality. The significance and value of the development of science cannot be held apart from the moral advancement of man; both imply the superiority of man morally and scientifically to his given situation.[17] This superiority is his ability to draw the consequences from the given situation and to direct these consequences into new realms of possibilities.

The virtue of truthfulness opens the present to the future. The progress of self-consciousness is based upon self-knowledge.[18] Thought is accountable to thought as the self; being accountable to the self transcends itself in accountability. It is in this accountability, *Rechenschaft*,

---

wuerde, dass er sich selbst doch immer nur ein Problem bleibt."

[13] *Ethik*, p. 508: "Die Wahrhaftigkeit fordert die theoretische Erkenntnis als die Grundlage der sittlichen Erziehung."

[14] *Ethik*, p. 508: "Dadurch allein wird die Ethik selbstaendig der Religion gegenueber."

[15] *Ethik*, pp.512–13: "Die Wahrhaftigkeit ist in der Logik begrundet; dieser Grund kann nicht ersetzt werden. Wo dieser Grund separiert oder vernachlaessigt wird, da wuchert die Phantasie . . . der Zusammenhang der Erkenntnisse bleibt die Wahrheit."

[16] *Ethik*, pp. 514–15: "Die Wahrhaftigkeit wird demzufolge aber auch zur Tugend der Philosophie, und zwar in dem Sinne, dass sie den Wegweiser bildet fuer die Wissenschaften in dem stetigen Gange sittlicher Arbeit, die in ihnen selbst sich volizieht und ohne welchen sie den Fortschritt der sittlichen Kultur nicht zu bewirken vermoechten."

[17] Rotenstreich, p. 191: "This is clarified thusly: Man's superiority ultimately amounts to his capacity to take a critical stand towards the present and to his power to envisage the horizon of the future." See also p. 192: "Man's release from the present harbors the seed of a planned transcendence of the event or the self-transcendence of man."

[18] *Ethik*, p. 519: "Die Tugend gilt als Wegweiser fuer die stetigen Fortschritte des Selbstbewusstseins."

that the given is surpassed and overcome. This accountability is necessitated by philosophical truthfulness and is characteristic of the essence of an *a priori* and idealistic ethics.[19] Reason and accountability form the *Logos*, and it is through accountability that the *Logos* emerges as reason. Ethics and science are based on identical principles of thought. The virtue of truthfulness embodies obligation and duties equally to theoretical and practical knowledge. There can be no exclusive obligation to one excluding the other; truthfulness embraces the two.

Truthfulness creates a disposition and a moral feeling which merge in a power to do homage to the ideal. To act with confidence and trust, with a sense of vivacity and joy, belongs to the essence of truthfulness.[20] We are aware that we are merely conditioned beings and can be subjected to the yet unconditioned, or should be. In truthfulness every conditioned being posits its self-criticism, its accountability, its self-transcendence. The virtue limits our efforts to absolutize the conditioned, limits our absorption in it, and opens it to its negation.

Truthfulness is the virtue of totality; through this virtue our individuality manifests and embodies the thinking of reason, *Denken der Vernuft*. The destruction of hedonism and mythology, Cohen's two chosen antagonists, is ascribed to the thinking of reason. The struggle against these antagonists becomes characteristic of Cohen's fidelity to reason and his devotion to the purity of the will. The purity of abstraction, the purity of the categorical imperative, the purity of the obligation of truthfulness to the laws of thought, and finally the truthfulness demanded in accountability, *Rechenschaftablegen*, all seem to reflect the purity of Cohen's religiosity as background and source of this philosophic thought. The oneness of methodology—the unending stress and demand for totality, the strict methodological parallels in logic, ethics, and aesthetics—gives the impression that Cohen gave himself the task of revealing the truth of monotheism in an all-inclusive way. The truth of monotheism is unique and absolute, excluding polytheism and anthropomorphism, not only in a religious sense, but more fundamentally in philosophical methodology. It is with this presupposition that Cohen continues his analysis of the virtues.[21]

The second virtue that Cohen considers is modesty, *Bescheidenheit*.

[19] *Ethik*, p. 516: "Der Apriorismus und Idealismus der Ethik bedeutet nichts anderes als die philosophische Wahrhaftigkeit."

[20] *Ethik*, p. 527: "Die Wahrhaftigkeit . . . ist in erster Linie die Kraft, welche mein Handeln regsam und lebendig, freudig und getrost macht. Die Wahrhaftigkeit ist die Kraft, welche die Sprache zum Bekenntnis erhebt; und das Bekenntnis laesst die Einsicht zur Ueberzeugung erstarken."

[21] *Ethik*, p. 532: "Die Wahrhaftigkeit hat das Selbstbewusstsein zu foerdern als das Selbstbewusstsein der Allheit. Ein Glied, welches sich ausserhalb der Allheit stellt, ist nicht mehr als ein allgemeines Glied derselben zu betrachten und zu behandeln."

This virtue is closely linked with truthfulness and posits its limits. Cohen introduces this virtue by identifying it with Socratic irony, a sense of limitation or productive ignorance. Truthfulness can be exaggerated into dogma unless freed by negative moment, a liberating scepticism. It is for the virtue of modesty to preserve in the search for truth the emphasis upon the logic of search, i.e., the polarity of irony. Its movement from positive to negative and again from negative to positive embodies its refusal of both sophism and dogmatism and reveals the essence of the virtue of modesty.[22] Here we have a disposition of thought, a strength of will needed to complement the virtue of truthfulness and the absolute form of its demand. The duty of modesty necessitates reference to the concrete and the inadequate, the contingent and accidental. It is in these conditioned situations that truthfulness must not only have its limitations, but against which it must always measure its abstractions and their universal and absolute nature. Between truthfulness and modesty there must be dialogue.

Cohen exemplifies this with contrasting statements of love and honor. In love I see the other in myself; in honor I see myself in the other.[23] Love, Kant had said, must be taken as a maxim of benevolence expressed in beneficence. Love draws men together, while respect demands distance. It is in love that we are closer to human inadequacies and failings, while the distance that respect demands enhances human dignity and the ideal of man. Cohen relates modesty to love, and from this it is possible to conclude that modesty stands to truthfulness as love stands to honor.[24] It is in modesty that we take into account the nature of our achievement both moral and intellectual and subject it to evaluation from which a degree of irony must never be lost. It is this irony which releases us from the bonds of the present and injects that meaningful doubt into our attempts to dogmatize our moral behavior. Irony, for Cohen, is thus a characteristic element of freedom. The irony of this freedom implies both acceptance and a transcendence in the same act.[25]

Modesty is the virtue which Cohen believes raises the most serious barrier to the aphoristic style. Although he does not mention Friedrich Nietzsche, it is apparent that Nietzsche's aphoristic style was repulsive to

[22] *Ethik*, p. 536: "Aber diese Negation (die Ironie) ist unerlaesslich. Ohne sie kann das Selbstbewusstsein nicht vor Ueberspannung und Ueberhebung geschuetzt werden. Die Bescheidenheit ist daher die Tugend der Skepsis."

[23] *Ethik*, p. 538: "Bei der Ehre soll ich mich selbst zunaechst nur im Anderen sehen; bei der Liebe dagegen sehe ich den Anderen zunaechst in mir."

[24] *Ethik*, p. 538: "Die Bescheidenheit wird zu einer kontrollierenden Instanz der Wahrhaftigkeit, wie der Affekt der Liebe zu dem der Ehre."

[25] See the discussion of freedom in Rotenstreich's *Spirit and Man*, chap. VI, e.g., p. 192: "For the utilization of the given implies, beyond attachment to the given circumstances, interference in the course of events."

Cohen.[26] Scientific thinking developed and unfolded, required analysis and synthesis, while the aphorism was a sudden revelation and its repetition was like moving from spark to spark.[27] The aphoristic thought is the conclusion of philosophy, the end of its development, the anarchy which announces the loss of faith and value in the coherent discourse. The virtue of modesty is expressed in style, but in one that is adequate to the philosophic virtue of truthfulness. This style reflects the process of reason, or the thinking of reason, both in its freedom and its law.

From style Cohen turns to the related problem of the hero and heroism; it is to virtue of modesty that we owe our rejection of the hero.[28] In the hero, the sense of irony is lost; dogma and the aphoristic style develop fully, but even more dangerous is the concomitant upsurge of myth. It is in myth-thinking, be it in terms of the state or in individuals, that the thinking of reason encounters its greatest barrier. In myth there is no longer that Socratic irony so helpful in warding off all absolutisms; there is no longer that humor which Cohen regarded as a safeguard against the extremes of optimism and pessimism. How little humor could be found in a Schopenhauer or an Eduard von Hartmann! The dangers of myth are always deeply perceived when the struggle is begun for a theory of human dignity and a political society under law because here the contrast emerges between atavism and humanity. Myths elevate heroes, national destinies, cultural superiorities, to the detriment of the universality of the categorical imperative.[29] Ernst Cassirer, pupil of Cohen, in his last book, *The Myth of the State*, pointed to the growing danger of myth in our century, echoing Cohen's fears:

> It is beyond the power of philosophy to destroy the political myths. A myth is in a sense invulnerable. It is impervious to rational arguments; it cannot be refuted by syllogism. But philosophy can do us another important service. It can make us understand the adversary. . . . We should carefully study the origin, the structure, the methods and the technique of the political myths.[30]

[26] *Ethik*, p. 540: "Die Bescheidenheit laesst keinen Gelehrtenduenkel aufkommen, geschweige den Duenkel genialer Erleuchtungen und Offenbarungen."

[27] *Ethik*, p. 540: "Waehrend das wissenschaftliche Denken sich entwickeln, sich entfalten, sich einteilen, sich gliedern muss, wird durch den Stil des Aphorismus die Periode zerhackt, der Gedanke atomisiert."

[28] *Ethik*, p. 544: "Heroismus widerstreitet ebensosehr der Wahrhaftigkeit wie insbesondere der Bescheidenheit."

[29] *Ethik*, p. 544: "Die Bescheidenheit ist der Tugendweiser gegen diese hoechst gefaehrliche und widerwaertige Manier, in unserer historischen Zeit mit ihrer verschlungenen Bedingtheit Helden zu fingieren. . . ."

[30] Ernst Cassirer, *The Myth of the State*, 2d ed. (New Haven, 1961), p. 296. See also Dimitry Gawronsky, "Ernst Cassirer: His Life and His Work," in *Philosopy of Ernst Cassirer*, The Library of Living Philosophers, Vol. VI (Evanston, 1949). This article has excellent vignettes of Cohen in Marburg and of Cassirer's relations with Cohen.

If Cohen sensed the danger of myth to ethics, Cassirer was witness to the effects of these myths in the catastrophies of the twentieth century.

Cohen exemplified his position toward myth and heroes when he spoke of the "Carlyle Style." Cassirer devoted a chapter of *The Myth of the State* to Carlyle, "On Heroes, Hero-Worship." The mystification of knowledge, the emphasis upon feeling, passion, and that untranslatable romantic vocabulary with its cult of great men, create a concept of history in which the virtue of modesty no longer excercises its limiting effects and in which the fallacies of men and their dependence upon conditions are no longer shown. Modesty is the virtue of history, and Cohen requires that we investigate circumstances and influence, that we evaluate and weigh consequences, for only thus is it possible to avoid the worship of the mythic Odin or the great historical personages.[31] How perplexing to thought are the poetic outbursts of Carlyle, and what anarchy they bring to logical discourse cannot but be illustrated in the following remark of Carlyle: "Cannot we conceive that Odin was a reality? Error indeed, error enough: but sheer falsehood, idle fable, allegory aforethought,—we will not believe that our Fathers believed in these."[32]

If in Carlyle there was still that belief in great morals and a rejection of brute physical force, the style of his thought could offer few barriers to the degenerative consequences which his thought allowed. It is for this reason that Cohen extends the virtue of modesty to every aspect of moral and intellectual life. It is this virtue which necessitates the persistent and constant moral striving essential to the perpetuation of the progress and advancement of morality.[33]

Cohen had endeavored to relate the virtue of modesty to the nature of historical understanding. It is this particular virtue which draws us to the individual. Here the universal is not the determinant, but the individual, his milieu, both particular and general.[34] The historical situation, the apparent consequence of a multiplicity of causes, is the true genesis of the problem of causation.[35] The movement from particular to universal is a movement analogous to that of the relation of modesty to truthfulness: virtues of critique finding their limits in each other. It is this movement that reflects the rationality of historical data and is the source of its significance.

[31] *Ethik*, p. 548: "Die Bescheidenheit wird nicht irre an den Grossen des Geistes, wenn die Kritik ihre Schwaechen erkennt, den Zusammenhaengen nachforscht, welche die geschichtliche Voraussetzung ihrer Originalitaet bilden. Die Bescheidenheit muss zur Tugend der Geschichte werden fuer die Charakteristik der Helden."

[32] Thomas Carlyle, *On Heroes and Hero Worship* (New York: Everyman's Library, 1965), p. 263.

[33] *Ethik*, p. 549: "Die Tugend bewaehrt sich als der Wegweiser fuer den stetigen Fortschritt der sittlichen Arbeit und der Selbsterziehung."

[34] *Ethik*, p. 551: "Sie [Bescheidenheit] sieht den Menschen immer in seinem allgemeinen und besonderen Milieu."

[35] *Ethik*, p. 551: "Du glaubst zu schieben, und du wirst geschoben."

This emphasis upon the individual and the particular characterizes Cohen's opposition to historicism and dialectical materialism. The disposition and strength of the virtue lie in its persistent affirmation of the individuality and the particularity of the historical situation. The material itself is the constant guide for historical knowledge.[36]

If in conclusion we summarize the virtue of modesty, there can be no better starting point than the opposition to all attempts to absolutize knowledge or to dissolve the problem of knowledge into poetry, aphorism, or mystical incantations. This virtue is the strength of reason against philosophies of feeling and passion which Kant already had declared to be dangerous to the philosophical undertaking. Cohen a century later could ponder the implications of the "Carlyle style" or the "Nietzsche Style," and although their authors had not yet seen the degenerative effects, the source of their possibilities was already provided. For ethics the threat was serious, and if the myth, the hero, or the mythologies could not be encountered by philosophy—for no discourse is here possible—then the task of philosophy remains: to point to the implications of mythical thinking and to enlarge the realm and significance of the virtues as constitutive of the disposition and will necessary to rational thought. The faith in reason depended upon the strength of the virtues.

The third virtue is courage, *Tapferkeit*. If truthfulness and modesty were intellectual virtues, courage is the virtue of the senses.[37] It is the actual struggle and the power to resist desire and lust; courage is the ability to forge the work of culture, *Arbeit der Kultur*. Cohen speaks of Prometheus as the ideal man who challenges the arbitrariness of Zeus and brings the possibilities of knowledge to man. For this he suffers the revenge of Zeus, but he knows that someday the god will be destroyed and his suffering alleviated. Prometheus is a symbolic figure capable of making us aware of the distinctive impasses and undermining forces latent in the work of culture. Kant had already made a profound discovery when he spoke of "beauty as the symbol of morality" in paragraph 59 of the *Critique of Judgment*: the extension of thought through symbol and analogy widens the scope for the applicability of morality. Promethean courage is perhaps not the destiny of all men, but in its sublimity our moral feeling is matured. Inseparable from this courage is the

[36] Nathan Rotenreich, *Between Past and Present* (New Haven, 1958), p. 208: "Hence the rationality of history is to be found in the fact that the material itself guides knowledge not only in terms of detecting and understanding its meaning but also in terms of the structure of the data."

[37] *Ethik*, p. 559: "Die Tapferkeit ist dem sinnlichen Menschen die sinnliche Tugend, die Kraft der Sinnlichkeit. . . . Die Gewalt, welche der Mensch ueber die Sinnlichkeit, ueber alle Arten und alle Richtugen der Sinnlichkeit errungen und behaupten kann, sie wird zur Tapferkeit. . . . Und die Tapferkeit ist gegen die Lust vorzugsweise gerichtet."

hope that the work of culture will succeed.[38]

Cohen speaks of a courage in suffering, *die Tapferkeit im Leiden*, in the suffering of work.[39] It is a courage beyond pessimism and optimism; it is a courage which reveals the human destiny to be beyond the tragic both ideally and concretely. Courage is for Cohen the virtue needed to bring forth the humanistic socialism in which he believed: a socialism which could emerge only with the alleviation of poverty and a meaningful concept of justice in a government under law; a socialism which would be manifest not only in national politics, but in world politics. The virtue of courage makes it possible not only to dream such a socialism, but to suffer in the work for its realization. Not only to project an idea of world history, but to act in its behalf is the virtue of courage: the courage for political action.[40]

It is clear that Cohen in his discussion of the virtues faced the dangers of exaggerated and extreme dispositions. Courage can degenerate to blindness and violent surges of behavior. Always present are the vices of asceticism and martyrdom, the fantasies of the Nordic myths, and the philosophies of aphorisms and cosmic pessimisms. Courage as virtue belongs to the history of mankind in terms of morality, as one realization of the dignity of man. In a degenerative way courage freed from this end can effect disdain and contempt for the idea of humanity. Courage is the virtue of the senses; disdain for the physical reality of man to the glory of the spiritual does violence to every aspect of communal life which accepts and develops a concept of justice.[41] Ethics, Kant has said, is concerned with the reciprocal duties among men, not angels or ascetics. It is for this reason that Kant was deeply interested in education, in experimentation in education and pedagogy. "Man can only become man by education. He is merely what education makes of him" (*Education*, p. 6). To turn away from the responsibilities which men have to each other is to surrender to ascetism or to martyrdom. In Cohen's language it is to renounce our obligation to the advancement of culture. "Martyrium und Asketik gehen haeufig zusammen im Bunde

[38] *Ethik*, p. 561–62: "Es ist Menschenlos, zu leiden, und im Leiden den Menschen auszubilden und auszupraegen. . . . Das tragische Leiden bedeutet und vollzieht die Tapferkeit . . . die den inneren Widerstand bildet, in dem die Kraft des Sieges beruht."

[39] *Ethik*, p. 536: "Die Tapferkeit im Leiden und in der Arbeit, im Leiden der Arbeit bringt die Loesung des tragischen Konfliktes im Menschendasein."

[40] *Ethik*, p. 563–64: "So ist die Tapferkeit der Wegweiser der politischen Taetigkeit; so wird sie zur eminenten politischen Tugend."

[41] *Ethik*, p. 566: ". . . dass er [dieser Heldenmut] sich nicht von dem Grunde geistiger Freiheit und Klarheit erhebt. Er ist haeufig nur der Ausdruck and der Gipfel einer Befeindung der Natur und der Sinnlichkeit, welche zugleich mit dem Mistrauen gegen die menschliche Sitte verbunden ist."

gegen die Kultur."[42] His opposition to hero morality and superman morality is climaxed in Cohen's comparison between this type of morality and devilry.[43] It is a morality "beyond good and evil," a revival of the old sophistic doctrine of the superman and the glorification of the identification between might and right.[44] In all this Cohen saw the destructive forces of a brooding pessimism that had renounced moral faith and resigned itself to the romantic illusions of mythological powers. The dogmatics of materialism grow when rational faith declines. Courage is a virtue in the strength of the will to advance the thinking of reason.

Cohen concludes that hero morality and myth-thinking are renewed expressions of attempts to absolutize the senses and a return to a new barbarism.[45] Courage, on the other hand, is the virtue of Idealism, *die Tugend des Idealismus*. It is the belief in the moral predisposition of man and the rejection of naturalism and hedonism. It is courage that gives us a position in relation to the world, and this is vital to meaning. Kant puts it this way in *The Strife of Faculties*:

> If the course of human affairs seems so senseless to us, perhaps it lies in a poor choice of position from which we regard it. Viewed from the earth, the planets sometimes move backwards, sometimes forward, and sometimes not at all. But if the standpoint selected is the sun, an act which only reason can perform, according to the Copernican hypotheses they move constantly in their regular course.[46]

Absent from the *Metaphysical Principles of Virtue* is a particular discussion of the virtue of faithfulness, *Treue*, but Kant had already linked faithfulness to a moral *credo* which he had delineated in an essay written for the Royal Academy of Science in Berlin in 1791. The essay is

[42] *Ethik*, p. 566. "Martyrdom and asceticism often are in league against culture."

[43] *Ethik*, p. 567: "Die Herrenmoral ist nichts als Teufelei."

[44] *Ethik*, p. 567: "Auf diesem Naturalismus, der wie unausrottbar scheint, beruht es im letzten Grunde, wenn der altsophistische Gedanke des Uebermenschen, der das Recht und die Sittlichkeit zu einer List des Staerkeren macht, immer wieder auftauchen und als Weisheit beachtet werden kann." In connection with Cohen's passionate opposition to this superman morality was his hatred of Wagner and his love of Mozart, in particular *The Magic Flute*. See "Mozarts Operntexte," in *Schriften zur Philosophie und Zeitgeschichte*, I, 490–519: ". . . es ist der hoechste Ruhm Mozarts, dass er das Ideal der *Ethik* in seiner Oper verherrlicht hat" (p. 514).

[45] *Ethik*, p. 571: "Die absolute Anerkennung der Sinnlichkeit ist ein Rudiment aus dem Stande der Wildheit."

[46] *The Strife of Faculties*, English trans. E. Fackenheim (Indianapolis, 1963), p. 141. *Der Streit der Fakultaeten*, part II (Weischedel, VI, 355): "Vielleicht liegt es auch an unserer unrecht genommenen Wahl des Standpunktes, aus dem sir den Lauf menschlicher Dinge ansehen, dass dieser uns so widersinnisch scheint. Die Planeten, von der Erde aus gesehen, sind bald rueckgaengig, bald stillstehend, bald fortgaengig. Den Standpunkt aber von der Sonne aus genommen, welches nur die Vernunft tun kann, gehen sie nach der Kopernikanischen Hypothese bestaendig ihren regelmaessigen Gang fort."

Kant's evaluation of the history of philosophy from Leibniz and Wolf to his own time and the place of his critical philosophy in this history.[47] Kant divides the moral *credo* into three articles: (1) I believe in one God as the source of all goodness in the world and as the ultimate purpose of this world. (2) I believe in the possibility, so far as it is in man's power, to harmonize this ultimate purpose with the highest good in the world. (3) I believe in a future eternal life as the condition of an ever-constant approach of the world to its highest possible good.[48] This moral *credo* is a faith in the pure practical reason, the moral faith in its efficacy and veracity. This is a faithfulness to a truth which is developed through constancy and endurance.

Cohen had made clear the dangers of hero-worship and superman philosophies for ethics, while it is in friendship and its implication that we get the first illustration of the virtue of faithfulness. Kant had spoken of the possibilities of moral friendship but had concluded on a pessimistic note. For Cohen friendship is an original form, *Urbild*, of human love and assurance that the moral substance of man is no illusion.[49] Faithfulness is the guide, *Wegweiser*, to friendship which, characterized by a steadfastness, *Bestaendigkeit*, is a fundamental form of moral self-consciousness. What is fundamental in friendship is not the mutual relationship, but the strength of the relationship, and this strength is faithfulness.[50] Friendship is more than I or thou, it is the virtue of faithfulness.

The virtue of faithfulness is the genesis of marriage: a natural relationship becomes a moral relationship; the arbitrariness and the commodity-nature, *gleich als Sache*, of the relationship are transformed by the law of humanity into the form of the eternal union of mankind.[51] The trust of love is for Cohen the essence of marriage—a faith in the

[47] "Welches sind die wirklichen Fortschritte, die die Metaphysik seit Leibnitzens und Wolfs Zeiten in Deutschland gemacht hat?" (Weischedel, vol. III).

[48] *Ibid.*, p. 636: "Daher hat der Glaube in moralischpraktischer Ruecksicht auch an sich einen moralischen Wert, weil er ein freies Annehman enthaelt. Das Credo in den drei Artikeln des Bekenntnis der reinen praktischen Vernunft; Ich glaube an einen einzigen Gott, als den Urquell alles Guten in der Welt, als seinen Endzweck;—Ich glaube an die Moeglichkeit, zu diesem Endzweck, dem hoechsten Gut in der Welt, so fern es am Menschen liegt, zusammenzustimmen;—Ich glaube an ein kuenftiges, ewiges Leben, als der Bedingung einer immerwaehrenden Annaeherung Dieses Credo, sage ich, ist ein freies Fuerwahrhalten, ohne welches en auch keinen moralischen Wert haben wuerde."

[49] *Ethik*, p. 579: "In der Freundschaft glaubt man die Buergschaft dafuer zu erkennen, dass die Menschheit, die Sittlichkeit kein leerer Wahn sei. Die Freundschaft erscheint als das Urbild der Menschenliebe."

[50] *Ethik*, p. 582: "Nicht in der Verbindung der zwei Menschen liegt die Erhoehung, sondern in der Bestaendigkeit dieser Verbindung."

[51] *M.d.S.*, p. 278: ". . . der Ehevertrag kein beliebiger, sondern durch Gesetz der Menschheit notwendiger Vertrag . . ."; also *Ethik*, p. 587: "Man sieht, nicht wegen der Ehe ist die Treue zu fordern, sondern der Treue wegen muss die Ehe da sein; waere sie nicht da, so muesste sie erfunden werden."

human relationship and its moral substance. This identification between trust and faith which Cohen here stresses reveals also his attitude toward religion. Religion is a means, a condition to advance morality, and insofar as this condition is justified, we can legitimize religion. The latter grows to a moral maturity only when it is incorporated into ethics. To the degree that religion embodies a moral substance, to that degree we accede to its right to be a source for the work of culture.[52] Cohen refuses to recognize the religious as a valid dimension of the human experience. It is at this point that the weight of Wilhelm Herrmann's argument becomes decisive. To dissolve the religious into the ethical is to deny it a right which it has claimed for the ages; the consequence of this denial is an absolute faith in reason both theoretical and practical.

It is the dross of myth, *Schlacken des Mythos*, that encumbers religion and conceals its ethical content. This utter opposition to myth-thinking and its close affinity to religion seems to explain Cohen's less than sympathetic attitude toward any religious thought not fully immersed in morality.[53] Wilhelm Herrmann, although critical of Cohen, in matters of religion nevertheless speaks of Cohen's personal attitude and disposition for the religious and his sincere attachment to the faith of Israel. In Cohen's letters this is apparent—in particular, the often-cited letter to Leo Munk in which Cohen speaks of his deep emotional attachment to the faith of his Fathers.[54] While it is obvious that Cohen's attitude is rooted in a deep repugnance to myth and mythologies, this appears to be the negative contrast preparatory to the yet-to-be-written religion of reason showing the significance and meaning of Judaism as the religion in which the moral substance is most perfectly preserved and revealed. This thought was already emerging in Cohen's article written in 1907, "Religion und Sittlichkeit," in which religion is distinguished sharply from myth and the uniqueness of the God of Israel is absolutely differentiated from the gods of mythology.[55]

[52] *Ethik*, pp. 591–92. Two examples of Cohen's position: (1) "Sie [Ethics] kann daher die Religion nur als einen Naturzustand anerkennen, dessen Kulturreife in die Ethik faellt." (2) "Die Religion muss als Mittel gebraucht werden, die Ueberfuehrung der Ethik in die allgemeine Kultur vorzubereiten."

[53] *Ethik*, p. 492: "Die Idealisierung der Religion geht dagegen immer darauf aus, von diesen Schlacken des Mythos sie zu reinigen und die ethischen Motive, die in ihr schlummern und die in ihr lebendig sind, klarer herauszuarbeiten und zu reiner Fruchtbarkeit entbinden."

[54] *Briefe*, p. 77: "Naples, 3. 27. 07. Sie wissen wie sehr ich mit den tiefsten Regungen meines Herzens und den innigsten Gefuehlen meines Geistes mit dem inneren Leben unserer Religion verknuepft bin. . . ."

[55] "Religion und Sittlichkeit," in *Juedische Schriften*, III, 122: ". . . die Goetter und Gott. Die tiefste Kluft, welche in der gesamten Kultur zu erspaehen sein duerfte, trennt diese beiden Begriffe von einander." See also p. 126: "Damit ist die Religion entstanden; die Religion im Unterschiede zum Mythos."

The virtue of faithfulness is thus fundamental on all levels of life, from the individual in marriage, to the relation of children to parents. There is a faithfulness to the community, to the state, and finally to mankind. Faithfulness transforms the externality of obligation into personal conviction and surety.

Justice is the virtue of the ideal state. Its ideality is embodied in the perfection of its form; concepts are inadequate for the representation of this state. Justice being the virtue of the ideal becomes the virtue of eternality.[56] The ideal of the just state is the expression of the task which political thought and action must assume. Although the just state belongs to the power of the imagination, it necessitates and posits the political discourse. This discourse contrasts the contemporary state with the just state, the state of vested interests, power groups, and class domination with the state of justice, *Rechtsstaat*.[57] The ideal makes every level of political thinking unsatisfactory because each level from family to state must ultimately recede before political thinking on the world level. Justice is universal; it should control and dominate all national and group dimensions. It does not level them, but from them the wider problems emerge; without them there would be no genuine universal problem.

In the *Metaphysical Elements of Justice*, Kant separated legality and morality:

> The mere argument or disagreement of an action with the law, without regard to the incentive of the action, is called legality; but when the idea of duty arising from the law is at the same time the incentive of the action, then the agreement is called the morality of the action.[58]

Cohen sees justice as the fundamental virtue of the state. In terms of the state as ideal, the legality and morality of action are fused by the accord which the ideal imposes. Kant throughout the *Metaphysics of Morals* had avoided introducing the state as an ideal. He spoke of the ideal of the juridical association of men, of the ideal of humanity in its moral perfection, of the ideal of virtue as its own end eclipsing holiness, of the differentiation between the ideal and the idol, of the ideal of virtue as unattainable and yet to be approached, of the dangers of those who

[56] *Ethik*, p. 621: "So wird die Gerechtigkeit zur Tugend der Ewigkeit."

[57] *Ethik*, p. 622: "Der empirische Staat ist freilich der Staat der Staende und der herrschenden Klassen; er ist nicht Rechtsstaat. Nur dadurch kann der Machtstaat Rechtsstaat werden, dass er das Recht, der Idee des Staates gemaess, nicht im Interesse der Staende und der Klassen ausbildet."

[58] Ladd, p. 19, *M.d.S.*, p. 219: "Man nennt die blosse Uebereinstimmung oder Nichtuebereinstimmung einer Handlung mit dem Gesetze, ohne Ruecksicht auf die Triebfeder derselben, die Legalitaet (Gesetzmaessigkeit), diejenige aber, in welcher die Idee der Pflicht aus dem Gesetze zugleich die Triebfeder der Handlung ist, die Moralitaet (Sittlichkeit) derselben."

think fantastically about achieving an ideal which can only be approximated.[59] From the ideal no particular can be derived or deduced, but we have an archetype, a standard which is indispensable for the defects latent in the actual state. So significant and dominant is the virtue of the ideal, of justice, that without this particular virtue Cohen is ready to declare all the others valueless.[60]

Cohen had dealt with justice in his *Kants Begruendung der Ethik*. In this book he commented upon Kant's definition of justice in the first part of the *Metaphysics of Morals*. In fact, he quotes Kant's definition and reaches similar conclusions:

> (1) Every action is just [right] that in itself or in its maxim is such that the freedom of the will of each can coexist together with the freedom of everyone in accordance with a universal law.
>
> (2) . . . if a certain use of freedom is itself a hindrance to freedom according to universal laws then the use of coercion to counteract it . . . is consistent with freedom according to universal laws.[61]

To be free from the constraint of another's will and assuming it does not limit the freedom of that other, is the innate equality demanded for all men—an innate equality rooted in innate freedom. Cohen calls this the eternal unwritten law, *das ewig ungeschriebene Recht*, which is the basis of the ideal of virtue. In this law the framework for an independent science of law is given. Inseparable from the unwritten law is the projection of the future state, *Zukunftsstaates*, the state of justice. It is an ideal which can in no way be identified with an existing state.[62] It is always the *should be* only to be approached or approximated. It is in the state as educator that we become aware that what exists must be transcended. It is in the state and through the state, as an educational process, that what exists loses its permanency and fixity and becomes the source of its own negation. The ideal redeems the state and political life from the demonic fixity which would be its fate without the demands of the *should be*. It is the virtue of justice which forces and necessitates us to keep apart and contrasted the eternal nature of the ideal and the relative, inadequate nature of historical reality.

[59] Ladd, p. 129, Gregor, pp. 57, 65, 71, 98, 102; see also Kant, *Critique of Pure Reason*, trans. N. K. Smith (New York, 1950), "Transcendental Dialectic, " Book II, chap. III, sections I and II.

[60] *Ethik*, p. 621: "Ohne die Gerechtigkeit aber wird alle Tugend wertlos."

[61] *K.B.E.*, pp. 403, 404, cited from *M.d.S.*, pp. 230, 231; Ladd, pp. 35, 36.

[62] *Ethik*, p. 606: "Das Problem vom besten Staate ist zugleich das Problem vom besten Recht. Beide sind Bilder, positive Utopien. Die Gerechtigkeit ermuntert nicht zu dem Bilde eines zukunftsstaates. Der Staat des Rechts ist als Staat der Zukunft in dem Ideal des Staates und des Rechts enthalten."

If it is justice which imposes the constant task of separating the historical from the eternal by means of the ideal, justice must also overcome the scepticism and sophism concerning the efficacy and truth of the moral law in us. Nothing could be more destructive to morality than the effects of these doubts of the moral law. Kant in the conclusion to *The Metaphysical Elements of Justice* states:

> Even if the realization of this goal of abolishing war were always to remain just a pious wish, we still would certainly not be deceiving ourselves by adopting the maxim of working for it with unrelenting perseverance. Indeed, we have a duty to do so, and to assume that the moral law within us might deceive us would give rise to the disgusting wish to dispense with reason altogether and to conceive of ourselves and our principles as thrown in together with all the other species of animals under the same mechanism of nature.[63]

The options of *Machtstaat* or *Rechtsstaat* belong conceptually to man. Cohen, like Kant, refuses to submit to a fate which the early sophists had identified as the might–right formula. Human destiny belongs to man if we assume the possibility of freedom. Moral faith in the moral law, the doctrine of virtue and the ideal are various expressions of the human responsibility. The violence introduced by doubt would silence the moral discourse and end the moral purpose of man.[64] If we assumed that the moral could deceive, then another world would be open to us. Not only would power politics be right because it is, but the world of myth and mythology, aphoristic and romantic philosophies would prevail, the pessimism of Schopenhauer and of von Hartmann could be given credence, and Mozart would yield to Wagner. Cohen believed that the virtue of justice, as the virtue of the ideal, did not imply or designate a pious wish or goal, but declared the reality of the practical reason and its categorical command and that we must act *as if* the justice of the *Rechtsstaat* existed. It was not an eudaemonian dream or fantasty, but an ideal of the imagination necessary to the moral law. The work of man is infinite, and if the ideal is never achieved it is perhaps the nonachievement that preserves for us the moral problem.[65]

[63] Ladd, p. 128, *M.d.S.*, p. 355: "Und wenn das letztere [end of war] wa die Vollendung dieser Absicht betrifft, auch immer ein frommer Wunsch bliebe, so betruegen wir uns doch gewiss nicht mit der Annahme der Maxime, dahin unablaessig zu wirken, denn diese ist Pflicht; das moralische Gesetz aber in uns selbst fuer betrueglich anzunehmen, wuerde den Abscheu erregenden Wunsch hervorbringen, lieber aller Vernunft zu entbehren und sich seinen Grundsaetzen nach mit den uebrigen Triebklassen in einen gleichen Mechanismus der Natur geworfen anzusehen."

[64] *Ethik*, p. 621: "Als die Tugend des Ideals erhebt sie auch ueber alle Skepsis und alle Schlaffheit des konservativen Opportunismum, fuer dessen Weltklugheit der Glaube an eine neue Welt eine ideologische Illusion ist."

[65] E. Weil, p. 138: "L'homme, être fini, peut et doit progresser indéfiniment, mais son

Cohen concludes his study of the virtues with the term *Humanitaet*, which approximates the Greek term *Sophrosyne* (practical wisdom). Cohen correctly states that the word is untranslatable, *nicht zu uebersetzen*, but some definition must be hinted at:

> The major premisses of conduct are certain universal judgments as to what is good for man in general, or as a rule: as to what ought to be done by such and such classes of people. In the major premisses the man of practical wisdom formulates his ideal—the true ideal. It is only a man who is in a healthy emotional state who can see the truth of such general principles when they are formulated. If his "moral sense," his taste has been perverted by wrong training, he fails to see the principle: he does not see, for example, why he should sacrifice his pleasure for the welfare of his neighbors.[66]

We can speak of moral insight and measure. When we speak of "seeing" in terms of action, we indicate an immediate apprehension of necessary action. We "see" that something has to be done; the focus is on the particular action, and it is directed to the individual.[67] The concern is with what can be done in the present. Cohen refuses to permit speculation about the future to lessen present responsibility. It is this practical wisdom that pointed to the dangers for moral freedom inherent in atavism and racism. These dangers were the new naturalism which called itself nationalism and threatened to undermine the concept of state as a moral and educational institution.[68] It was this new naturalism, joined by myth-thinking, hero-cults, and aphoristic philosophic styles that made Cohen identify the concern for the individual with the concern for the minority.[69] The possibility of the survival of the Jew could hardly be imaginable where such a naturalism became dominant and the concept man became "a mere superficial, abstract quality." In this respect, Hegel, classical in expression, would claim that the state misunderstood its basic principle. Hegel's remark in the *Philosophy of Right* is significant:

> But the fierce outcry raised against the Jew [as belonging not merely to a religious sect, but to a foreign race] . . . ignores the fact that they are, above all, *men*, and manhood, so far from

progrès doit rester progrès, ne doit jamais s'arrêter, il ne doit pas y avoir de repos pour l'être moral."

[66] H. H. Joachim, *Aristotle, The Nicomachean Ethics: A Commentary* (Oxford, 1951), p. 211. See *Die nikomachische Ethik* (Zurich, 1967), 1140b, 16–20, 1142a, 23–30.

[67] *Ethik*, p. 635: "Die Humanitaet ist aber schon dadurch von der Idee der Menschheit unterschieden, dass sie vornehmlich auf das Individuum selbst sich richtet."

[68] E. Weil, *Philosophie politique* (Paris, 1966), p. 245. "Au risque de choques, il faut dire que la théorie antique (arostotélienne, en particulier) de l'Etat comme institution morale et éducation est vrai."

[69] *Ethik*, p. 634: "Die Humanitaet wird dieser Notwendigkeit gegenueber [rule of the state by the majority] zum Anwalt der Minoritaeten."

> being a mere superficial, abstract quality is, on the contrary itself the basis of the fact that what civil rights arouse in their possessors is the feeling of oneself as counting in civil society as a person with rights . . . it [the state] would have misunderstood its own basic principle, its nature as an objective and powerful institution.[70]

The struggle against the falsification of man as the subject of morality and the distortive definition of state implied a practical wisdom which Aristotle called *Sophrosyne*.[71] The two basic characteristics of the virtue, the "eye" for the particularities of the situation and the peculiarity of individuals, invest our action with a universality that corresponds to the universal principle of the will.[72] The universal demand of the moral law has its source in the objective moral situation. The contrasting modes of universality and particularity reflect the rational structure of the state in which these modes seek their unattainable reconciliation. The naturalism which Cohen perceived to be developing in the ideologies of the European states of the nineteenth century threatened to destroy the contrasting modes of rationality from which the rational state could possibly arise. The states of Europe, naturalistic in their nationalism, were in violation of the concept of the state, the consequences of which were documented in the twentieth century.

The concept of the particular, *der Begriff des Besonderen*, is inexhaustible; there is no reconciliation of universal and particular, there is approximation.[73] The particular is the inexhaustible, refusing redemption and absorption in political or economic ideologies. It is the foundation of the legal state. The whole educative process of state must seek to destroy those myths and cults created by religion and the nation to justify its

[70] Hegel, *Philosophy of Right*, trans. T. M. Knox (Oxford, 1949), p. 169n. Hegel, *Grundlinien der Philosophie des Rechts* (Hamburg: Meiner Verlag, 1955), par. 270, note: ". . . so sehr hat das aus diesen und anderen Gesichtspunkten [e.g., the Jews are a foreign people] erhobene Geschrei uebersehen, dass sie zu allererst Menschen sind und dass dies nicht nur eine flache, abstrakte Qualitaet ist, sondern, dass darin liegt, das durch die zugestandenen buergerlichen Rechte vielmehr das Selbstgefuehl, als rechtliche Personen in der buergerlichen Gesellschaft zu gelten. . . . Die den Juden vorgeworfene Trennung . . . denn er [the state] haette damit sein Prinzip, die objektive Institution und deren Macht verkannt."

[71] Felix Weltsch, *Das Wagnis der Mitte* (Stuttgart, 1965). *Sophrosyne* could imply prudence or measure, avoidance of extremes. This book is a philosophy of measure, the third dimension between the extremes; for does not man essentially belong to this third dimension? "Der Mensch ist ein Wesen der Mitte . . . in dem Sinn, dass seine metaphysische Situation und seine weltanschauliche Stimmung den deutlichen Charakter der Mitte tragen" (p. 168).

[72] *Ethik*, p. 636: "Das scharfe wohlwollende Auge fuer die Besonderheiten des Falles, fuer die Eigenart der Personen, die dabei in Frage kommen, bibt dem Blicke Umsicht und Umschau."

[73] *Ethik*, p. 624: "Das Besondere aber ist unerschoepflich."

historical hatreds and its self-glorification. The virtue of practical wisdom embodies the strength to expose and to root out these aberrations.[74] The ideal of the rational state embodied the ideal of virtue as *Humanitaet*. Cohen spoke of this *Humanitaet* as the law of moral harmony, the harmonizing power for all the melodies of the moral spirit, *die harmonierende Macht fuer alle Melodien des sittlichen Geistes*. This was Cohen's answer to the Treitschke dictum: "The Jews are our misfortune." The misfortune could only be in the denial of the concept of particularity and in the affirmation of an all-embracing naturalistic nationalism. Cohen struggled to forge a philosophy of values grounded in the universal-categorical dictates of reason that could counter an historicism capable of justifying the ideologic and mythologic historical thinking of contemporary politics. The virtue of *Humanitaet* regards man not merely as a natural being, but as an animal endowed with reason.[75] This is the virtue of *Menschengefuehl*, the feeling for the human. In the animality lie the finiteness and imperfection which make the struggle for truth and morality both beautiful and sublime, but accompanied with pain. We are limited by our conceptual power; life surpasses comprehension but is confirmed in our trust of the human, *Menschengefuehl*.[76] It is this feeling which links aesthetics to ethics and is the source of great art because it affirms in man the humanity of his person as the ideal of beauty. Great art, as Kant reminds us, "requires a union of pure ideas of reason with great imaginative power even in him who wishes to judge of it, still more in him who wishes to present it."[77] In Cohen's language, the art of the ideal is the art of humanity.[78] In this feeling for the human in its particularity and finiteness lies the source for a concept of humanity. The progress of civilization is rooted in diversity and pluralism, and the virtue of *Sophrosyne*; the feeling for the human, *Menschengefuehl*, deepens our awareness of this and impels actions that deny

[74] *Ethik*, p. 633: "Bald ist es die Religion, welche Scheiterhaufen anzuendet, bald ist es das Vaterland, welches den Hass der Fremden zur Pflicht mache; immer werden Vorwaende gesucht und gefunden, um die Kraenkung der Menschlichkeit zu entschuldigen und beschoenigen. Die Humanitaet allein vermag alle jene Irrgaenge der Kultur unwegsam zu machen."

[75] *M.d.S.*, p. 456: ". . . weil hier der Mensch nicht bloss als vernuenftiges Wesen, sondern auch als mit Vernunft begabtes Tier betrachtet wird." Insofar as man is an animal he is limited and imperfect. It is in terms of these modes of finiteness that the virtue of *Humanitaet* comes forth as the feeling for the human, *Menschengefuehl*.

[76] *K.d.U.*, p. 309: ". . . denn nur soviel sieht man vollstaendig ein, als man nach Begriffen selbst machen und zustande bringen kahn." See also *Ethik*, p. 638: "Humanitaet ist urspruengliches Menschengefuehl; nicht Urteil ueber den Wert des Menschen. . . . Was waere alle Tugend, wenn sie dieser urspruenglichen Mahnung misstrauen und entsagen muesste."

[77] *K.d.U.*, p. 60: ". . . dazu gehoeren rein Ideen der Vernunft und grosse Macht der Einbildungskraft in demjenigen vereinigt, welcher sie nur beurteilen, viel mehr noch, wer sie darstellen will" (Bernard, p. 72).

[78] *Ethik*, p. 641: "Die Kunst des Ideals ist so gewiss die Kunst der Menschheit."

and oppose the atavistic myths of religion and politics which separate, in hate, man from man and nation from nation. Cohen in his *Tugendlehre* reflects a conflict of values that nineteenth-century Europe had seen sharpened by the development of nationalism and its chauvinistic social and religious consequences. In Cohen, as in Kant, we realize the shortness of our lives and the weight of the moral task; it demands moral faith and a belief in the future, the strength of virtue and a bit of irony. Kant expressed the historical dimension of the development of man's capacity to use reason in a way which makes us aware that the heritage of reason belonged, belongs, and hopefully will belong to mankind as a responsibility. Its development requires time: "Since Nature has set only a short period for his life, she needs a perhaps unreckonable series of generations, each of which passes its own enlightenment to its successor in order finally to bring the seeds of the enlightenment to that degree of development in our race which is completely suitable to Nature's purpose."[79]

The virtues are the guides and the ideals; upon them Cohen placed his faith in the future. This was a moral faith, a moral feeling, a moral hope.

[79] Immanuel Kant, *Idee zu einer allgemeinen Geschichte in weltbuergerlicher Absicht* (1784), in *Kleinere Schriften zur Geschichtsphilosophie Ethik und Politik* (Hamburg: Meiner Verlag, 1959): "Zweiter Satz . . . wenn die Natur seine Lebensfrist nur kurz angesetzt hat, so bedarf sie einer vielleicht unabsehlichen Reihe von Zeugungen, deren eine der anderen ihre Aufklaerung ueberliefert, um endlich ihre Keime in unswerer Gattung zu derjenigen Stufe der Entwicklung zu treiben, welche ihrer Absicht vollstaendig angemessen ist." Eng. trans., *On History* (Indianapolis, 1963), p. 13.

Chapter III
THE ETHICS OF JUDAISM IN COHEN'S PHILOSOPHICAL THOUGHT

Eight years after the publication of the second edition of the *Ethik*, Cohen published a book that dealt specifically with the concept of religion: *The Concept of Religion in the System of Philosophy.*[1] The criticism of Wilhelm Herrmann indicating both Cohen's failure to handle adequately the problem of religion in his ethics, and the apparent conflict between his personal religious beliefs and his published writings, made it necessary for Cohen to come to grips with the problem of religion. Herrmann had pointed to Cohen's brochure "Religion and Morality," published in 1907, as an attempt in this direction.[2] It was, however, in 1915 that Cohen for the first time devoted himself in detail to the problem. Cohen's works were never devoid of religiosity, and although they were critical of the myths and mythologies advanced by folk religions and dangerously prevalent in more highly developed European religions, they showed deep attachment to the purity of monotheism and to the prophetic demand for justice. There was, however, no indication that Cohen was willing to subordinate ethics to religious faith, or that he was inclined to substitute theophany for the autonomy and spontaneity of reason. There was in Cohen a religiosity as there was in Aristotle, Spinoza, and Kant, but it was as yet without religion. The question that now arises is whether Cohen's publications from 1907 to 1919 reveal a religiosity with a religion. We have discussed the problem of virtues in the *Metaphysics of Morals* and in Cohen's *Ethics of the Pure Will*;

[1] *Der Begriff der Religion im System der Philosophie* (Giessen, 1915), henceforth referred to as *B.d.R.* The book was dedicated to the Marburg School. Cohen had left Marburg in 1912 and settled in Berlin.

[2] From 1907 to 1915 Cohen published several articles dealing specifically with the problem. The significant articles are: (1) "Religion und Sittlichkeit" (1907), *J.S.*, vol. III; (2) "Innere Beziehung der Kantischen Philosophie zum Judentum" (1910), *J.S.*, vol. I; (3) "Die Liebe zur Religion" (1911), *J.S.*, vol. II; (4) "Die Lyrik der Psalmen" (1914), *J.S.*, vol. I. Meaningful was the effect that Eastern Jewry made on Cohen during this period. See his article "Der polnische Jude," *J.S.*, vol. II. Although this article was published in 1916, Cohen had made the trip to Poland and Russia in 1914 and published his views in the same year. See Note to "Der polnische Jude," *J.S.*, II, 474.

Cohen takes up the problem again in his last work, *Religion of Reason*, and by comparison we can indicate that changes of direction have taken place. And if a change is indicated, is it not already marked in the *Concept of Religion*?[3]

The third chapter of this book is called "The Relationship of Religion to Ethics" and introduces almost immediately the concept of correlation, *Korrelation*. Not God alone, nor the Unmoved Mover of Aristotle, nor the pantheistic religiosity of Spinoza, but God in correspondence with man through revelation and creation opens the human sphere to the divine.[4] If, as Cohen states, religion begins when man stands alongside the divine, the question arises, how do we come to know this God? Kant had already posited the question of the ultimate end of creation.[5] This moral faith expresses the moral attitude of reason. It is based on the laws of freedom, not subject to theoretically determinant judgment, but is knowledge for the practical cognition, *die praktische Erkenntnis*. Cohen now states that what the good is, God will reveal. This he affirms through the declaration of the prophet Micah: "It has been told thee, O Man, what is good."[6] The good is the transformation of man into humanity; it is the anticipation of the future, a messianic humanity; it is the answer to the Kantian question, what may I hope for?—*Was darf ich hoffen?* This messianic hope, this trust in the future of humanity, *die Zuversicht auf diese Zukunft der Menschheit*, is embodied in the dogma of a particular religious tradition, and in the very use of this tradition Cohen implies that he accepts it and, as a philosopher, he will attempt to reconcile or to approximate this specific tradition with the moral law and with the moral faith which he had expounded in his previous writings.

[3] In the history of thought the struggle between philosophy and religion may be expressed in the contrast between *Sophrosyne* as Cohen had analyzed it in his *Ethics of the Pure Will* and what Gershon Scholem says about religious values: "There is then a scale of values that have been taken over from tradition; there is also a group of doctrines and dogmas, which are taken as authentic statements concerning the religious experience of a community. And there is a body of rites and customs, traditionally believed to transmit the values and express the mood and rhythm of religious life." *On the Kabbalah and Its Symbolism* (London, 1965), p. 6.

[4] *B.d.R.*, p. 32: ". . . nicht Gott allein und an sich sondern immer nur in Korrelation zum Menschen, wie freilich daher auch gemaess der Korrelation: nicht der Mensch allein, sondern immer zugleich in Korrelation mit Gott."

[5] *K.d.U.*, par. 83 note; also, "Allgemeine Anmerkung zur Theologie," p. 468. The distinction must be made between *Endzweck* and *letzter Zweck*, which I have translated as ultimate end and final end. Emil Fackenheim in his valuable article "Kant's Concept of History," *Kant-Studien*, 1956-57, p. 391, n. 28, states: "We use the term 'end-in-itself' for Kant's 'Endzweck' which we carefully distinguish from 'final end' ('letzter Zweck'). A 'final end' is the final achievement of nature toward an 'end-in-itself' which, if for no other reason than it is an end-in-itself, transcends nature."

[6] Bible texts are from *The Soncino Books of the Bible* (London, 1909), *The Twelve Prophets*, Micah, VI, 8. *B.d.R.*, p. 33: "Was das Gute sei, soll der Gott verkuenden."

This messianic religion explicates a new concept of time; the past and the present are subordinated to the future, but only in terms of anticipation. The anticipation of the future is a truth already revealed and confers upon the past and the present a transcendent unity which mere historicity could never provide.[7] But in this Cohen moves sharply away from his ethics and the virtue of practical wisdom, for there the present was dominant and Cohen was critical of futuristic speculations. We are, however, dealing with contrasts and not oppositions, aiming not at reconciliation, but at evaluations in terms of contrasting values and accentuations.

If we reflect upon the last chapter of the *Ethik*—its discussion of the concept of the particular, the distinction between the abstract individual (*das Einzelne*) and the concrete individual (*der Einzelne*), the emphasis on the present, the unity of the virtues in practical wisdom (*Sophrosyne*)—it is difficult to discover where religion can enrich ethics. Wilhelm Herrmann had rightly said that Cohen's conclusions are Kant's conclusions; God as a living reality suffers extinction in the purity of the postulate.[8] Although Cohen reaffirms his position that religion can have no greater purpose than to enrich ethics, he is equally aware that religion raises questions which he had not considered in ethics. Had not the prophets, in particular Jeremiah and Ezekiel, discovered that individuality and sin are so closely related that no definition of the individual is possible without consciousness of sin?[9] The purity of the monotheistic principle was the guarantor against all the myths and atavistic attributes that still infested the contemporary religious scene; it was the guarantor of universalism and the ideal of law as categorical against historicism, relativism, and materialism. But this God of ethics must relate to the individual personally, and if he is a sinner there must be postulated forgiveness or the hope in forgiveness. The religiosity which belongs to ethics must yield to religion which speaks concretely about sin, prayer, and hope. Cohen had already derived from religion, from an historical religion, the messianic future; he was now to derive from it the meaning of the individual as morally fallible.

The new concept of man, *der neue Begriffe des Menschen*, Cohen

[7] *B.d.R.*, pp. 33-34: ". . . so wendet sich die Religion des Messianismus ab von der Vergangenheit und der Gegenwart; ein neuer Zeitbegriff wird von ihr fuer den Menschen in Korrelation zu Gott geschaffen: die Zukunft. Sie allein erfuellt die Zeit, sie allein macht die Zeit lebend, wahr und gehaltvoll." For an evaluation of the concept of messianism from a contemporary scholar, see Gersom Scholem's article "Zum Verstaendnis der messianischen Idee im Judentum," in *Judaica* (Frankfurt am Main, 1968), pp. 7–75.

[8] *B.d.R.*, p. 42: "Denn wie konnte die Religion mehr verherrlicht werden, als wenn ihre Aufloesung in die Ethik ihr eigenes Ziel gennant wird? Ich habe die methodische Konsequenz nicht gescheut, dass die Religion in Ethik sich aufloesen muesse."

[9] *B.d.R.*, p. 56: "Und die Ethik hat von der Religion gelernt, dass die Propheten, besonders Jeremiah und Ezekiel, an der Selbsterkenntnis der Suende das Individuum erst zur Entdeckung brachten."

discovers in the significance of three terms: sin, redemption, and reconciliation.[10] With these terms we stand at the beginnings of religion. These beginnings are not historical; they are primordial, analogous to the negation of privation, the origin of the finite from within the infinite.[11] These beginnings are the very assumption of the religious dialogue as they are of the moral and the theoretical. But Cohen is not yet inclined to give religion an independence and continues to affirm that the extension of the problem only enriches ethics.[12] Nevertheless, if for Cohen correlation is the uniqueness of religion, and the prophetic linkage of sin and individuality necessitates a new concept of man, this new concept would also imply a new knowledge of God. If religion posits a God whose uniqueness transcends all conceptualization, then it must also transcend ethics, and this Cohen admits.[13] Cohen had known the intimacy of intellectual beliefs that exists between man and moral ideas and which is so vital to ethics. This inadequacy of abstraction, *die Maengel der Abstraktion zu beseitigen*, didn't express the uniqueness of religion in terms of longing and trust in the divine.[14] There was a uniqueness in the relation between God and man; historical religion had spoken of God as the redeemer from whom man sought redemption. A degree of individuality is achieved in the divine–human correspondence which ethics does not reach in its analysis of either irony or of prudence. The affirmation of God is the path to forgiveness of sin. Cohen rejects any attempt, however, to make God a helper or a source of absolution from the moral obligation. The moral law commands unconditionally, and God does not change its legislative force; He is its truth, and forgiveness is in this truth. The truth that is loved must in no way destroy or hinder the autonomous moral activity of the lover of this truth.[15] It is the moral substance that God affirms as truth and thus confers holiness on the moral activity. The belief

[10] *B.d.R.*, pp. 57–58: "In diesen positiven Momenten vollzieht sich der neue Begriff des Menschen, den die Erkenntnis vom sittlichen Mangel und von der Suende herbeigefuehrt hat."

[11] *B.d.R.*, p. 58: "Wir stehen am begrifflichen Ursprung der Religion." For the mystical side of this problem, see Gershom Scholem, "Schoepfung aus Nichts und Selbstverschraenkung Gottes," in *Eranos-Jahrbuch*, vol. 25 (Zurich, 1957).

[12] *B.d.R.*, p. 58: "Im grunde ist es gar kein Uebergang, der hier bevorsteht, sondern innerhalb der Ethik selbst vollzieht sich diese Erweiterung des Problems und Loesung."

[13] *B.d.R.*, p. 61: "Die Einzigkeit aber faellt ganz aus dem Rahmen der Ethik heraus. Hier muss der Ueberschritt zur Religion eintreten."

[14] "Die Lyrik der Psalmen," *J.S.*, I, 253. "Die Sehnsucht ist nur das Mittel, die Maengel der Abstraktion zu beseitigen, die Gewissheit dem persoenlichen Bewusstsein nahezubringen; aber im letzten Grunde soll nur diese Gewissheit als Zuversicht lebendig gemacht, als Vertrauen persoenlich gemacht werden."

[15] *B.d.R.*, p. 63: "So wenig die Erloesung ein Gnadengeschenk Gottes sein kann, ebensowenig kann sie das Produkt seiner Mitwirkung bei der sittlichen Arbeit sein, ueber die das Wesen Gottes hinausliegt."

in God is the affirmation and acceptance that He loves the activity of man, for whom moral law is command and faith. It is not *as if* the moral law is divine commandment, but the *belief* that it is a divine commandment, that changes the direction from ethics to religion. The use of the analogy is for the ethical argument; it strengthens the moral incentive but in no way implies an obligation to a God. Rather, it deepens the moral obligation which man places on himself and from which he alone understands himself as moral subject.[16] In the assumption of correlation, Cohen necessitates an obligation to God, who can no longer serve merely to explain purposiveness in nature, but who is the source of moral obligation and who forgives our fallibility while not lessening our moral responsibility.[17]

The uniqueness of Judaism is the purity of its monotheism. It was apparent in Cohen's discussion in his *Ethik* that the pantheisms and mythologies which he feared were latent in Christianity were absent in Judaism. The purity which he sought in logic, in ethics, and in aesthetics was analogous to the purity of monotheism. For in this alone lay the denial of myth, anthropomorphism, and the doctrine of grace which threatened to diminish the moral substance. The worthiness for redemption, *Wuerdigkeit zur Erloesung*, accentuates worthiness over redemption. The uniqueness of God calls forth the uniqueness of man as the moral subject. The reality of this God is manifested in the moral activity which He induces and requires. The religious arises from the challenge to transform the profanity of life through the moral worth of action into the ideals which the virtues delineate. The "moral law within me" and the "starry heavens above me" are not simply objects which fill the mind with "awe and admiration" and belong to the aesthetic feeling. They correspond with the revelation of God awakening in us an awareness of our moral destiny. There is a moral heroism in this response to the divine command that has its roots in the trust in divine redemption.[18] In Christianity Cohen was disturbed by the incarnation because its factual historical form threatened to end the inseparability between the divine and the human and implied a pantheistic motive that Cohen had always seen as dangerous to a religion that endeavored to preserve the sanctity of morality.[19] In the abstract purity of

[16] *M.d.S.*, p. 444: "In diesem [praktischen] Sinn kann es also so lauten: Religion zu haben ist Pflicht des Menschen gegen sich selbst."

[17] *B.d.R.*, p. 64: "Der Mensch bleibt in der Arbeit, aber Gott, der an dieser Arbeit selbst nicht teilnimmt, wird als das Wahrzeichen gedacht, das die Befreiung von der Suende Bewirkt."

[18] *B.d.R.*, p. 67: "Dieses Idealbild des menschlichen Individuums ist nicht das Schreckgespenst seiner Verzweiflung, sondern das Heldenbild seines Ringens ueber seine menschlichen Grenzen hinaus, aber verklaert durch die Zuversicht der Erloesung, die ihm von jenseits dieser Grenzen der Menschheit entgegenleuchtet. . . ."

[19] *B.d.R.*, p. 67: "Only a symbolic Christ, the ideal of morality could save Christianity from pantheism and preserve for it an ethical center." "Der pantheistische Doppelsinn, der die zweite Person der Gottheit umscheiert, wird allmaelich abgestreift, und die

monotheism—although it meant a great loss in terms of popular religion, with its necessary anthropomorphism and mythology—the ultimate irreconcilability between God and man could be maintained and its consequences for ethics clearly affirmed.

At the end of the chapter Cohen raises that delicate problem of suffering. He had considered this problem in his *Ethik* together with the virtue of courage, *Tapferkeit*. The suffering which attended life was interwoven with an anticipation of a future realization of humanity. The individual becomes aware that his suffering and the collective moral struggles of men are necessary for the moral self-consciousness that emerges from these struggles and the realization that the work of culture is guided by a courage that has been in sharpest contrast with all doctrines of pessimism.[20] Again in the *Concept of Religion* Cohen affirms that suffering must not be the cause of pessimism. A metaphysics of pessimism does violence to ethics and to religion; messianism in all its ramifications would be nullified, for the trust and hope from which it is built would be doubted and questioned.

The suffering of the guiltless is the new problem for Cohen, the undeserved suffering of the just.[21] And it is with this question that Cohen raises the greater and perhaps more incomprehensible world-historical question—that of the suffering of Israel, her exile and her redemption.[22] Although this problem has been the genesis of both profound and sublime myths and symbols, Cohen's immovable attachment to the moral law limited his speculations to the moral meaning and significance of Israel's suffering, but derived from it the idea of a messianic humanity that drew together moral and religious faith. The problem is not only a world-historical one, but some of its profoundest moments concern the individual. The suffering of the pious, *das Leiden des Frommen*, tears apart the demonic connection that has been made between sin and suffering. The suffering of the pious drives us beyond the definitions of man as *Endzweck*, as final end, beyond the dignity of man to a human greatness which correlates man to God in the supreme work of creation. It is in this work of creation that the deepest suffering is accepted. The realization of a moral universe and of moral man emerges in these sufferings of love. God will redeem the pious as they redeem His

menschliche Person Christi wird fuer die lebendige Arbeit der Religion in den Mittelpunkt gestellt."

[20] *Ethik*, p. 561: "Die Tugend der Tapferkeit erledigt die ganze sogenannte Metaphysik des Pessimismus. . . . Das Leiden ist da, diese Tatscahe ist in ihrem vollen Umfange anzuerkennen; aber sie ist nicht als Pessimismus zu deuten." See other pertinent text, pp. 560–63.

[21] *B.d.R.*, p. 74: ". . . wie kann Gott das Leid der Frommen verantworten?"; and the further question, ". . . wie kann es dem Gerechten schlecht gehen?"

[22] *B.d.R.*, p. 74–75: "Sie bildet vielleicht ein Grundkapitel in aller Philosophie der Geschichte: das Leiden eines Volkes fuer ein anderes oder fuer andere Voelker. . . ."

world. This is a religious odyssey with radiating moral consequences; the love of God now implies the burden of bearing goodness into the world.[23]

It is important to inquire into the justification for these religious interpretations which Cohen makes, and to ask about the authority he ascribes to these sources. In his final chapter, "Religion in Relation to Psychology," he states:

> Religious sources may teach me but they cannot give authoritative direction. One can only explain and justify the interpretation of the moral law as God's command from the point of view that I, out of my own reason, from autonomy, accomplish it. I do it because I want to define, create and ground religion.[24]

Statements such as these point to the inconclusive position which Cohen still maintained in 1915. The constant return to a Kantian position makes it impossible to claim that Cohen had finally subordinated his Kantian heritage to Judaism, a claim vindicated only in his final work. It was in that work that a synthesis was reached between Judaism, Plato, and Leibniz, and Cohen emerged with a new metaphysics.

Cohen appears convinced that ethics and religion are so inseparably linked to each other, and that this constitutes the uniqueness of Judaism, that if an attempt is made to absolutize one at the expense of the other, the mutuality in which they are rooted would be lost. Religion cannot assume that the autonomy of the moral task can be ameliorated by doctrines of grace which obviate the moral responsibility that ethics categorically affirms, even though religion discovers and extends into new realms the dimensions of individuality and deepens the divine–human confrontation. With God, the struggle and suffering of each man are meaningful and vital. Cohen, weighing the contrasts and parallels, attempts to write the script of ethics in religious terminology; it was the pure monotheism of Judaism that supplied the possibility of this terminology. Cohen viewed Judaism as the embodiment of that holy and sublime relationship between ethics and religion. What Kant had seen only in a particular instance, Cohen had seen as a general characteristic.[25]

[23] *B.d.R.*, p. 81: "Wenn ich Gott liebe, so denke ich ihn nicht mehr nur als den Buergen der Sittlichkeit auf Erden, sondern von der Allheit lenke ich den Blick ab ueber andere Former der Mehrheit hinweg auf diejenige Partikularitaet, welche den Armen als Beispiel der sozialen Partikularitaet aufhebt und schlechthin zum Individuum macht."

[24] *B.d.R.*, p. 117: "Die religioesen Urkunden koennen nur Belehrung geben, aber keine autoritative Anweisung. Die Deutung des Sittengesetzes, als goettlichen Gebotes, kann sich daher nur erklaeren und rechtfertigen aus der Ansicht, dass ich aus eigener Vernunft mithin aus Autonomie sie vollziehe. Und ich tue dies, weil und sofern ich Religion definieren, schaffen und begruenden will."

[25] *K.d.U.*, par. 29: "Perhaps there is no sublimer passage in the Jewish law than the command, 'Thou shalt not make to thyself any graven image, nor the likeness of anything

The final chapter of the *Concept of Religion* is a further expression of Cohen's belief that religion without ethics is either myth or dogmatic confession and that ethics without religion is embraced in abstraction.[26] The shift in Cohen's thinking implies that the isolation and loneliness, *Verlassenheit und Vereinsamung*, of moral knowledge, the creation of the moral world from the ego, the divine within me, now becomes a creation in correspondence, a creation within a correlation. Kant's moral thought had expressed philosophically what Luther had affirmed theoretically against thomistic realism: the idealism of faith and the freedom of the Christian man against the realist structure of the Church. Cohen was not untouched by Protestantism and admiration for the German Reformation, its radical Paulinism, and the subsequent Pietist heritage. His Kant was a son of Pietism, his colleague Lange was in the same tradition. Correlation, however, shifts the emphasis away from man. It does not place it exclusively in God, but lets it rest in the relationship itself in the *correspondence*. Cohen could state: "The totality by which one has to think of humanity does not guarantee individuality as such. For that I need God as my God. My own God is the God of religion."[27] But the God that commands is greater than the moral law in me, and although He is not contrary to it, the relationship between the moral law in me and the divine command outside me constitutes the new confrontation within the religio-ethical correlation. The human question might be religious, the obligation is always moral; forgiveness and love are the divine realities in which our individuality is released from the abstractness of the concept. In this God of religion there lies the assurance and the human response to it that ultimately goodness will be realized in this world.[28] Ethics is concerned with the source and application of moral

---

which is in heaven or in the earth or under the earth.' This command alone can explain the enthusiasm that the Jewish people in their moral period felt for their religion" (trans. Bernard, p. 115). "Vielleicht gibt es keine erhabenere Stelle im Gesetzbuch der Juden als das Gebot: Du sollst dir kein Bildnis mach noch irgendein Gleichnis, weder dessen, was im Himmel noch auf der Erden noch unter der Erden ist. Dieses Gebot allein kann den Enthusiasmus erklaeren, den das juedische Volk in seiner gesitteten Periode fuer seine Religion fuehlte." For Kant's relation to Judaism see: N. M. Graupe, "Kant und das Judentum," *Zeitschrift fuer Religion und Geistesgeschichte* (1961). Michael A. Meyer, *The Origins of the Modern Jew* (Detroit, 1967), p. 74, n. 50.

[26] *B.d.R.*, p. 83: "Aber alle Relativitaet und Partikularitaet bleibt mit der Abstraktion verhaftet: sie wird erst verscheucht durch den Ausgang der Besonderheit in das Individuum. . . . Aber erst die Religion bringt die Korreptur an dieser logischen Abstraktion an, insofern sie den Menschen als Individuum auszeichnet. . . ."

[27] *B.d.R.*, p. 116: "Die Allheit, als welche die Menschheit zu denken ist, verbuergt nicht die Individualitaet, als solche. Dazu bedarf ich Gottes, als meines Gottes. Mein eigener Gott ist der Gott der Religion."

[28] *B.d.R.*, p. 116: "Diese [the distinction between the God of ethics and religion] steht nur ein dafuer, dass es der Sittlichkeit niemals an der Menschenart mangelt, so dass die Sittlichkeit auf Erden sich nicht verwirklichen koennte."

principles. It could postulate the existence of such a God or the existence of a moral relationship with God. The fact that correlation is introduced means that Cohen believed that the religious relationship between man and God is a dimension of the human experience which is necessitated both by the failure of ethics to deal concretely with human fallibility and to offer the positive assurance of redemption that only the God of religion promises to the world and to man. Yet the God of religion is inseparably bound to ethics. Only in conformity to the autonomy of ethics can the God of religion be the God of the ethical man.[29] In a similar way it can be said that only within the ethical experience is the religious experience possible. These are conclusions which Cohen reaches in this book in his efforts to maintain that ethico-religious relationship that he believed so vital in the history of mankind.

It was only in the final pages of this book that Cohen turned from the problem at hand and considered the role of Judaism and Christianity. Cohen's career from 1879 to 1915 had never been without that confrontation between Christianity and Judaism.[30] In 1879 Treitschke had written a pamphlet, "A Word on Our Judaism," to which Cohen had replied in 1880, "The Jewish Question, a Confession." At this early period Cohen wrote: "We want to amalgamate physically with the German people. There must be no double nationality, no feeling of double loyalty."[31] Cohen at this period valued Judaism and Protestantism as allies of Kantianism in a struggle to preserve critical rationalism from skepticism and romanticism. Judaism in the *Concept of Religion* now occupies a unique position. The whole concept of religion is dependent on the unique monotheism of Judaism.[32] In this respect Judaism is the eternal center from which all other religions emanate; their truth or their falsity relates to their closeness or distance to this primordial truth.[33] In terms of the moral consequence of this monotheism, Cohen states that prophetic religion is its practical application and

[29] *B.d.R.*, p. 116: "Der religioese Gott ist nicht selbstaendig, sondern durch die Ethik bestimmt. Und nur im innigsten Anschluss an die Autonomie und nur unter ihrer strengsten Aufrechterhaltung kann der religioese Gott der Gott des ethischen Menschen werden."

[30] This confrontation was friendly and sincere with such colleagues as Lange, Herrmann, and Wellhausen, vicious with Paul de Lagarde, and hardly meaningful with Treitschke. See Hans Liebeschultz, "Hermann Cohen and Historical Background," *Leo Baeck Institute Year Book XIII*, 1968. J. Ebbinghaus, "Deutschtum und Judentum bei Hermann Cohen," *Kantstudien*, 60. Jahrgang, 1969. Michael Meyer, "Great Debate on Anti-Semitism: Jewish Reaction to New Hostility in Germany, 1879-1881," *L.B.I.Y.B. XI*, 1966.

[31] Cited in Hugo Bergman, *Faith and Reason* (Washington, 1961), p. 29.

[32] *B.d.R.*, p. 120: "Fuer alle Entwicklung der Religion aber muss der Begriff des einzigen Gottes der unveraenderliche Schwerpunkt bleiben."

[33] *B.d.R.*, p. 120: "Diese Schwerpunktes der Religion wegen muss das Judentum fuer alle Entwicklung der Religion das unerschuetterliche Fundament bleiben."

guide.[34] The pureness of this monotheism, its radical separation from cultic mythology, sexual perversion,[35] and other ceremonial sensualities, is analogous to the pureness of knowledge, pureness of will, and pureness of feeling. The prophets, in Cohen's view, mediate a divine experience whose authority spreads through the activities of men and set the goals and limits of what he had in the *Ethik* designated as the work of culture. It was, therefore, unacceptable to Cohen that Judaism was given a limited role in the history of religion by previous German thinkers, e.g., Lessing and Hegel, the consequences being that its historical role and fulfillment had occurred with the rise of Christianity and Islam.[36] This view Cohen encountered in his colleague Wellhausen, but the tradition was old and widespread in both Protestant and Catholic thought; it received greater emphasis, however, with the rise of the science of history in the eighteenth century and the concept of historical development. Cohen's avowed opposition to historicism would follow from any attempt to reduce reason to the category of historical development. The meaning of Israel is meta-historical and inexhaustible; the realization of the purity of monotheism has yet only begun; we are only at the beginnings of the religious odyssey as we are at the beginnings of moral consciousness.

The 53rd chapter of Isaiah was for Cohen the greatest wonder of the Bible: its imagery reflected the course of human history.[37] Cohen had begun to rewrite his ethics with biblical imagery and more concretely with the symbol of Israel as the suffering servant, the Messiah. It is evident that Cohen, in concluding this book with detailed and symbolic descriptions of Israel as God's servant, projects the peculiarity of religion in terms of the messianic future. It is difficult to find lacking in his *Ethik* many of the other factors which he ascribed to religion. It is the Messiah and Messianism that are crucial to Cohen in religion and are for him the essence of his faith in Judaism. It is in this messianic view that Cohen finally answers the criticism of Herrmann and would no longer find himself in that comfortable assimilationist position that he earlier had expressed to Lange. "What you call Christianity, I can call prophetic Judaism."[38]

The sufferings of the divine servant, the sufferings of the pious, make

[34] *B.d.R.*, p. 120: "Fuer die Entwicklung der Religion bleibt der prophetische Monotheismus der Wegweiser der Menschheit."

[35] *Ethik*, p. 634. Cohen realized the link between atavism and sexual perversity.

[36] See the study of Emil Fackenheim, "Samuel Hirsch and Hegel," in *Studies in Nineteenth-Century Jewish Intellectual History*, ed. A. Altmann (Cambridge, 1964), and N. Rotenstreich, *The Recurring Pattern* (London, 1963).

[37] *B.d.R.*, p. 128: "Das 53. Kapitel des Jesaja ist vielleicht das groesste Wunder des Alten Testaments. . . . Unter dem Gleichnis dieses Kapitels erscheint alle bisherige Geschichte in ihrem innersten Werden."

[38] Cited in Bergman, *Faith and Reason*, p. 28.

mockery of the popularly held bond between suffering and sin; the doctrine of reward and punishment has little meaning in this symbolism of the suffering servant. Suffering projects the heights and depths of man, but emerging from these sufferings of love is the messianic future; the pious in their suffering redeem the profane while they bear the uniqueness of God in the world.[39] It is the divine uniqueness that is the true burden, for without the pious the victory of evil would be assured. Cohen had spoken of the Promethean in his *Ethik*, but there the human heroism was in terms of man's self-sufficiency and the divorce from the gods; the pious, on the other hand, in the depths of suffering, their physical humility, affirm God and reject pessimism and skepticism. In Prometheus the victory over the gods is the aesthetic ideal of man; the suffering of the pious is the fulfillment of the correlation between God and man.[40] It is in this movement from man as *Endzweck* to correlation that indicates the shift in Cohen's thinking from the *Ethik* to the *Begriff*. The mediation of the uniqueness of monotheism is through correlation, and the subsequent sufferings of the pious are indeed the sufferings of love. This is not a cult of morbid suffering, for the messianic symbol of this suffering in Isaiah, and the eternal role of Judaism embodies the truth, without which both philosophy and religion would lose their legitimacy. This messianic role of Judaism incorporates that unique element of religion that differentiated it from ethics. The virtues, the problem of suffering, and the individual were all ethical problems, but in terms of the Messiah and in terms of the messianic future there is a new valuation, a transvaluation. Yet, it is in the work of man that the redemption of mankind occurs; religion is deeper in the feeling of the finite than in a cosmic or pantheistic feeling.[41] In this respect Cohen reached his sharpest opposition to Spinoza and Hegel. The redemption of mankind belongs to the individual activities of the pious reaching back through the ages, and it is from these same activities that God emerged as love and redemption.[42] Cohen is ready to concede to a mystic claim and declares that God longs for man as man has longed for God,[43] yet the concern has

[39] *B.d.R.*, pp. 127–28: "Das Leiden ist keineswegs die Strafe des Armen fuer Schuld und Suende, sondern die Unschuld wird verfolgt vom Leiden, und die Armen sind die Frommen, der Rest Israels, auf dessen Schultern die messianische Zukunft liegt."

[40] *B.d.R.*, p. 131. Cohen quotes from Isaiah—"He had no form nor comeliness, that we should look upon him, nor beauty that we should delight in him"—and compares this description with aesthetic ideal: "so drueckt der Prophet in diesem Idealbild seiner Menschlichkeit den Gegensatz zum aesthetischen Menschen-Ideale aus."

[41] *B.d.R.*, p. 134: "Paradox ausgedrueckt, wuerde die Religion vielmehr das Gefuehl des Endlichen sein muessen."

[42] *B.d.R.*, p. 134: ". . . dass der Mensch im Pantheismus vom All der Gottheit verschlungen und in seiner Individualitaet vernichtet wird. Die Rettung der Individualitaet ist aber die eigentliche Aufgabe der Religion."

[43] *B.d.R.*, p. 134: "Die Mystik hat es schon richtig gefuehlt, dass auch Gott nach der Kreatur schreit, wie diese nach ihm."

been to avoid all those tendencies that would permit any infringement upon the moral activity of man. Messianism is a fulfillment of the moral universe. God is the unique being; He is the unique center of being and thus the beginning and end of all true movement.[44] It is this uniqueness that posits the ultimate separation between God and man. All human activity toward God is only approach and approximation; there is no fusion and no identification; God is always the beyond. Our work and our reality are, therefore, always inadequate and incomplete. The deeper our awareness of this divine uniqueness, which is for Cohen the eternal message of Judaism, the deeper our liberation from earthly divinations and their demonic consequences.[45]

In 1919 Cohen's last work appeared. It is to this work that we turn for Cohen's final conclusion and to evaluate a history of thought that began in 1907 and ended in 1918. It is possible that the metaphysics that Kant had destroyed were revived by Cohen as he moved closer to the Judaism that embraced eternity and truth.

Behind Cohen's *Ethik* stood Kant, in the background of the *Concept of Religion* was the *Ethik*, embracing the totality of the tradition is the *Religion of Reason*. As each work of Cohen's must be read in terms of the others and all in terms of Kant, the study of particular aspects of Cohen's thought must presuppose this developmental approach, for without it the consequent fragmentation of thought would endanger a systematic evaluation.[46] By 1915 Cohen had reached the position that pure monotheism, the *Einzigkeit Gottes*, was inseparable from the "being or non-being of the moral universe" and that, therefore, our stake in the being of the moral universe was identifiable with our stake in Judaism.[47] Judaism is the guardian of a truth, the truth of the pure *Sollen* which characterizes the truth of religion and pervades the realm of moral philosophy. It is from this point of view that Cohen attempts to detail the

[44] *B.d.R.*, p. 137: "Die Korrelation ist nicht schlechthin Wechselverhaeltnis, sondern Gott wird ihr Schwerpunkt. In diesen Schwerpunkt wird das Sein verlegt."

[45] *B.d.R.*, p. 139. Cohen's concluding remarks restate his belief that this peculiarity of religion is to call attention to the moral consequences of the uniqueness of God. "Nur durch die Scheidung zwischen Gott und Mensch kann der Mensch die wahrhafte Ueberwindung dieser Welt erlernen, und zwar nicht etwa als Weltverachtung, sondern als Hintanstezung aller Gueter der Welt, aller irdischen Gelueste gegen das einzige Gut, welches das einzige Sein ist."

[46] In a similar vein Simon Kaplan's statement: "One must underneath the technical language, feel the passionate commitment to the work of reason and of ethics that speak out of these words, and out of the lives of Kant and Cohen if one wishes to understand this modern tradition at all." "The Day of Atonement," *Judaism*, Summer 1968, p. 353.

[47] *Religion der Vernunft* (henceforth *R.d.V.*), p. 272: "In dieser Frage [question of tolerance] gibt es kein Schwanken und keine gegenseitige sich bedingende und einschraenkende Anerkennung der Gegensaetze, sondern Sein oder Nichtsein der sittlichen Welt ist die grosse Frage." See also "Einheit und Einzigkeit gottes," *J.S.*, vol. I (1917).

world mission of Israel as the bearer of the religion of reason. It is only from the standpoint of this universal undertaking that the suffering of Israel is meaningful. It is not a suffering that bears identity to that of other political peoples; it is a suffering born from the uniqueness of its God. It is from within this framework that Cohen writes his *Religion of Reason—From the Sources of Judaism.*

Cohen devoted the last five chapters of his book to the problem of the virtues, but this problem could only be introduced by speaking of the attributes of God as the source of virtue. God alone is reality; He is more than the *monos* of monotheism; His otherness expresses His incomparableness; He is the unique truth.[48] God is no longer merely transcendence. He is the ground and source of reality, the origin of all that is: the origin of man and the world.[49] His being is holy, and from the holiness of His being proceeds man's obligation to become, to approach holiness. The Being of God is the source of man's becoming; the acknowledgment of the distinctiveness of God, the holiness of God, is the essence of the correlation, for in this acknowledgment lies the movement that characterizes man's acceptance of the responsibility to move toward the divine center. It is in this responsibility that man seeks forgiveness for his fallibility and prays for the "new heart." Prayer is the language of man's dialogue with God, a language expressive of that longing for truth that is the source of life. In prayer, all theory remaining in the correlation is removed and that intimacy and love so difficult to achieve in the universal structure of ethics is attained.[50] It is in prayer that the divine holiness is revealed as that pure *Sollen* that obligates and necessitates all human activity and is both its cause and its end. Inseparable for Cohen are the moral implication and responsibility which emerge from the correlation. The correlation posits an ontological and an ethical dimension: "In the former [the ontological] man is insured against the loss of the spirit since the spirit is of divine origin; with the latter [the ethical] man is enjoined to overcome sin through repentance, and through the moral dynamic of this redemptive process. . . ."[51] The concept of correlation reflects a profound

[48] *R.d.V.*, p. 480: "Wie Gott des einzige Sein ist, so ist er euch die einzige wahrheit. Denn Wahrheit ist das einzige Sein, das daher durch keinen anderer Geltungswert bezeichnet werden kann."

[49] Henry Slonimsky, "Hermann Cohen," in *Essays* (Chicago, 1967), pp. 97–112.

[50] *R.d.V.*, p. 463: "So ist das Gebet die eigentliche Sprache der Religion. Und alles Denken dieser Sprache, von Gott und vom Menschen, alles Denken dieser Korrelation bliebe Theorie, wenn nicht das Gebet die Sprachhandlung wuerde, in welcher der Wille lebendig wird an allen Mitteln des Denkens."

[51] N. Rotenstreich, *Jewish Philosophies in Modern Times* (New York, 1968), p. 96. See also *J.S.*, III, 189: "Der heilige Geist, von Gott dem Menschen gegeben, bildet den unzerstoerbaren Charakter des Menschen." *R.d.V.*, p. 119: "Durch den Geist ist jeder Mensch zur Heiligkeit berufen; an jeden Menschen ergeht das Gebot der Heiligkeit, und so will Gott auch durch jeden Menschen geheiligt werden."

optimism toward man's redemptive activity. God can be reconciled with His creation through human activity. The moral task of man is absolutized, and the moral faculty, divinely implanted, corresponds to the divine intention to redeem creation in repentance. On a cosmic level, the correlation between God and Israel reflects the truth of this redemption.

The virtues are an application of a truth that is God, the recognition of which is the source and origin of moral responsibility. The theophonous source of moral responsibility shifts the problem from the causative *woher und wodurch?* to the teleological *wohin und wozu?* The meaning and significance of man and world are ultimately embraced in messianic purposiveness; the anticipation of the future in hope and faith is that new time dimension in which drama of the ethical is composed. Monotheism has hardly begun to come forth. Its historical journey has only begun; the significance of Israel contradicts all the historical Christian schemes of the nineteenth century and their relegation of Israel's history to an already-exhausted and finished phase of world history. Cohen's remark in this respect is perhaps one of his most astounding.[52] The strength and the guides which are the virtues designate them as the significant factors in the realization of monotheism's breakthrough into world history. Monotheism is the truth; the virtues are the signs for its fulfillment.

The virtue that corresponds to the truth of God, to the ideal of truth, is truthfulness, *Wahrhaftigkeit*.[53] The God of truth necessitates truthfulness, and this virtue requires a constant cleansing of self. Truthfulness awakened the possibility of the divine human correlation, and it became the motto of Cohen's book: "Blessed are ye O Israel: before whom do ye make yourselves clean and who makes you clean? It is your Father in Heaven" (Akiba, Mishna, Yoma, end). Truthfulness was embodied in the persistence of the prophets to cleanse the divine service of all polytheism, anthropomorphism, and other elements that hindered and compromised the spirit of holiness that dwells between God and man.[54] Illustrative of this spirit is Psalm 51:19, "The sacrifices of God are a broken spirit; a broken and a contrite heart, O God, thou wilt not despise." The truthfulness of action and living is service in truth. In prayer, this truthfulness is transformed by

[52] *R.d.v.*, p. 184: "Die Weltgeschichte ist kaum erst angefangen noch nicht dreitausend Jahre ist sie alt seit Moses und den Propheten. Und so wird der Monotheismus seine Weltlaufbahn erst recht beginnen. Der Monotheismus ist der wahrhafte Trost der Geschichte." The truth of Judaism belongs to the future. The history of religions is the preparatory ground of its truth.

[53] *R.d.V.*, p. 482: "Welche Tugend nun entspricht der Wahrheit Gottes, dem Ideal der Wahrheit?" The virtues are now related to the truth.

[54] *R.d.V.*, p. 482: "Die Tugend der Wahrhaftigkeit ergibt sich nicht nur als Konsequenz von Gott als dem Gott der Wahrheit, sondern auch aus der ganzen prophetischen Predigt fuer den wahren Gottesdienst."

the psalm lyrics into the truth of prayer. Cohen had always been sensitive to style. For him it was characteristic of thought and faith. He rejected the Carlyle style, refused the aphorism as the style of systematic thought, scorned romantic sentimentality because he believed that each endangered the systematic employment of reason. The style of the Psalms is, however, derived from truthfulness and mirrors that constant demand for cleanliness and purity so vital to Cohen in every aspect of the human endeavor, i.e., from logic to prayer. Purity is basic to every aspect of Cohen's thought and comes to the fullness of its fruition in the correlation between God and man, for this correlation is in essence the eternity of the Kingdom, the meta-historical reality of Judaism, the embodiment of the truth of God. Not only is there a cleansing of the inner self, but under the "Yoke of the Law" the Jew negates the profanity of the world. The "Yoke of the Law" is the "Yoke of the Kingdom of God."[55] Separated from all the historical peoples, the Jews are for Cohen a destined people of faith, *dieses einzige Glaubensvolk*. From the God that is their truth emerges the truthfulness with which they hallow creation. In virtue of this religious truthfulness, the ethical man is the religious man.[56]

"Lo, it is a people that shall dwell alone, and shall not be reckoned among the nations" (Num 23:9), for this people must become a kingdom of priests, *Priesterreich*.[57] They bear witness to the messianic future when God will be Father and men will be brothers. The past has not known mankind, and in the present mankind has not yet awakened; the future alone is the source of this ideal of mankind.[58] Israel is the witness of this future. In her presence the messianic future is assured, for Israel is the suffering servant, the Symbol of the Messiah.[59] In Israel the truth of the future was the beginning. For men there is history; Israel is, however, totality. All this terminology is rooted in Cohen's basic belief in the truth that proceeds

[55] *R.d.V.*, p. 401: "So muss auch im Gesetz der Israelit das Joch auf sich nehmen; aber mit diesem Joch der Gesetze nimmt er zugleich auch das 'Joch des Gottesreich'. Es ist nur ein Joch: das der Gesetze und das des Gottesreich. Es gibt kein anderes Gottesreich als das Reich der Gesetze. Welches andere Reich koennte es geben?" For certain similar ideas in Franz Rosenzweig, see A. Altmann, "Rosenzweig on History," in *Studies in Religious Philosophy and Mysticism* (Ithaca, 1969), pp. 275–91.

[56] *R.d.V.*, p. 485: "Der sittliche Mensch ist kraft der religioesen Wahrhaftigkeit der religioese Mensch."

[57] "Das soziale Ideal bei Platon und den Propheten," *J.S.*, I, 330: "Das ganze Volk ein Priesterreich, dieser prophetische Grundgedanke muss die Losung der neuen Welt werden." This final lecture ended with the moving exclamation "But we are eternal." Franz Rosenzweig, "Einleitung," *J.S.*, I, lxii.

[58] *R.d.V.*, p. 292: "Die Menschheit hat in keiner Vergangenheit gelebt, und auch in keiner Gegenwart ist sie lebendig geworden; nur die Zukunft kann ihre Lichtgestalt heraufbringen."

[59] *R.d.V.*, p. 487: "Symbol wird das Volk endlich im Knechte des Ewigen, dieser Letzten Gestalt in der Symbolik des Messias. Den auch der Messias ist ein Symbol fuer die einheitliche Durchfuehrung des Gedankens vom einzigen Gotte."

from the uniqueness of the *monos* of God. Cohen's thought never degenerates into arbitrary symbol-play, nor is transcendence ever sacrificed for a temporality in which symbol becomes dogma.[60] The ethical substance of Cohen's thought is expanded and deepened by this belief in the Messiah, in the power of the Good, and in the certainty that the oneness of God will give forth into the oneness of humanity. The truthfulness of Israel's existence could hardly be justified if the significance of the chosenness of Israel were not transformed into the messianic mankind.[61] The community of Israel, under the Law, is not her isolation, but the transfiguration of the profane into the holy.[62] In this symbolic state Israel becomes the believing community, *die Gemeinde*.[63] The moral work of man is cloaked and embraced in religious terminology and symbols; the tradition of Judaism provides the armory which Cohen needs to unify the moral law with the oneness and distinctiveness of the God of Israel. The truthfulness of man remains his finiteness, and it is in this that his moral responsibility is unimpaired and the incomparableness of God is not weakened. The transformation of Israel's chosenness into that of the pious of the world is symbolic of the messianic task imposed upon the ethical endeavor:

> Whether any individual or any particular group has been elected by God, God himself alone knows; for man, election comprises an aim toward which he strives and a task wherewith he feels himself commissioned. God and God alone knows who belongs to the corpus mysticum.[64]

The truthfulness with which one bears this endeavor designates the pious; it is a truthfulness commanded by the truth of God, the two correlative moments of correlation. Truthfulness radiates not only toward God, but

[60] Kant's caution must be emphasized: the schematical and the symbolic must not be confused. *K.d.U.*, p. 258: ". . . so ist alle unsere Erkenntnis von Gott bloss symbolisch, und der, welcher sie mit den Eigenschaften Verstand, Wille, usw., die allein an Weltwesen ihre objektive Realitaet beweisen, fuer schematisch nimmt, geraet in den Anthropomorphismus."

[61] *R.d.V.*, p. 488: "Ohne diese Selbstverwandlung des auserwaehlten Volkes in die messianische Menschheit haette sich allerdings die juedische Wahrhaftigkeit schwerlich behaupten koennen."

[62] *R.d.V.*, p. 428: "Nicht die Isolierung ist der einzige Zweck des Gesetzes, sondern die Idealisierung alles irdischen Tuns mit dem Goettlichen. Der Gottesdienst beschraenkt sich nicht auf die Synagoge; das Gesetz erfuellt und durchdringt das ganze Leben mit ihm."

[63] *R.d.V.*, p. 449: "Die Gemeinde hat den Staat ersetzt. . . . Das Volk Israels ist die Gemeinde Israels geworden. Und hier ist auch das Wort fuer die Versammlungen in Gebrauch gekommen. Die gemeinde Israel Wuerde die Versammlung Israels."

[64] Hugo Bergman, "Israel and the Oikoumene," in *Studies in Rationalism, Judaism and Universalism* (London, 1966), p. 63. Although Cohen extended the symbol of Israel to include the pious of the world, he was sure that Israel was God's chosen people and that she was the one truth that passed through all history and annuls the divisions of time that lead to relativism and historicism. Her future anticipates the truth that was revealed in the beginning.

toward our fellow man, *Mitmensch*, and its affect is honor, *Ehre*, the equality that should exist among men. "Before God all men are equal." It is with this faith that Cohen rejects the vanities of the national heroes and myths of national and racial superiorities.[65] In the *Ethik* the struggle against these perversions was left to the moral faith in the moral law; here the concrete faith of a living religious tradition incarnates the moral faith into a religious one, and the consequent belief and trust in God enhance the strength and steadfastness of the moral effort. There was an optimism in Cohen that was lacking in Kant. Kant could have written the sixth thesis of *Idea for a Universal History* (1784) and said:

> He (Man, for he is an animal) thus requires a master, who will break his will and force him to obey a will that is universally valid, under which each can be free. But whence does he get his master? Only from the human race. But then the master is himself an animal, and needs a master.[66]

This optimism, or perhaps better stated, this assurance in Cohen of the reality of God, frees his work from any mood of resignation or even doubt. Even the irony so highly praised in the *Ethik* is absent in his final work. He believes in the messianic significance of the *Glaubensvolk*.

Truthfulness is an absolute virtue. It obligates unconditionally, but all unconditional necessitation must be moderated by the subjective condition of man. Only a relative virtue can moderate this absolute obligation; modesty, or *Bescheidenheit*, is such a virtue. It is this relative virtue that leads to humility, *Demut*, for what other stance can man afford before the great religious questions? Modesty and humility do not weaken the absolute nature of truthfulness, but deepen and enhance it. Truthfulness accompanied by modesty and humility reflects a profounder grasp of the truth that is God.[67] Cohen quotes: "Now the man Moses was very humble, above all the men that were on the face of the earth" (Num 12:3). It is in this humility that one bears witness to the awe of God, *Gottesfurcht*, and confesses subjection to His truth.[68] In the *Ethik* Cohen had identified humility with a

[65] *R.d.V.*, p. 496: "Vor Gott sind alle Menschen gleich. Da gibt es nicht hoch und niedrig."

[66] *On History*, p. 17; *Werke*, VI, 40: "Er bedarf also eines Herrn, der ihm den eigenen Willen breche, und ihn noetige, einem allgemein-gueltigen Willen, daher jeder frei sein kann, zu gehorchen. Wo nimmt er aber diesen Herrn her? Nirgend anders als aus der Menschengattung. Aber dieser ist eben so wohl ein Tier, das einen Herrn noetig hat."

[67] *R.d.V.*, p. 493: "Und dazu bedarf ich der Selbsterkenntnis der Bescheidenheit, die vor den grossen Fragen mich zur Demut fuehrt. Bescheidenheit und Demut werden so zu Helfern der Wahrhaftigkeit. In ihnen besteht die relative Tugend zur absoluten der Wahrhaftigkeit."

[68] *R.d.V.*, p. 493: "Die Demut allein schuetzt den Menschen vor der Gefahr des Stolzes auf seinen Menschenwert, der doch nur erst gegruendet wird in seiner Gottesfurcht, in seiner Unterwerfung unter die Wahrheit Gottes."

sense of one's unworthiness, while modesty was, on the other hand, a feeling of one's worthiness and dignity.[69] It might be asked if the *Gottesfurcht* does not in some way lessen the feeling of respect for the moral law in us as the awe of the divine fills us with humility. This shift in mood reveals the further movement of Cohen's thought toward the religious. Humility has gained the recognition which only a God of truth could confer and demand.

God loves the humbled; humility is the true sign of piety; humility before God becomes modesty before our fellow man. Humility now assumes a messianic dimension. The striving of each man and each people is toward humility. Not the hero, national pride, or atavistic naturalism fulfills the calling of man, but true wisdom and virtue are achieved only in humility. No age and no man is free of this obligation to the virtue of humility.[70] Highly illustrative of this humility is Peretz's story "Sontsha the Silent":

> "Really! I tell you [the divine judge], everything is yours. Everything in Paradise is yours. Choose! Take! Whatever you want!"
>
> "Well then, what I would like, Your Excellency, is to have, every morning for breakfast, a hot roll with fresh butter."[71]

The interplay of humility and modesty embraces the virtues that direct our obligations and form our maxims toward both God and man. Humility recognizes that the piety of life flows from the recognition that "all are of the dust, and all return to the dust"; this is the way that leads to God,

[69] *Ethik*, p. 554: "Darin liegt der Unterschied der Bescheidenheit von der Demut, dass sie das Gefuehl des eigenen Wertes festhaelt, waehrend die Demut mit der Fiktion des eigenen Unwerts operiert." In the *R.d.V.* humility has become the presupposition of the divine–human relationship. See p. 94: "Bei jeder Relation mit Gott ist Demut die Voraussetzung fuer den Menschen. Unter dieser Bedingung kann sich die Korrelation zwischen Mensch und Gott rechtfertigen."

[70] *R.d.V.*, p. 495: "Nichts anders kann sich der Beruf des Menschen, die Zukunft der Menschheit erfuellen als dadurch, dass jeder Mensch fuer sich selbst und jedes Volk fuer sich selbst nach Demut strebe. . . . Da gibt es keine Ausnahme, fuer keinen Menschen, fuer kein Volk und fuer kein Zeitalter."

[71] I. Howe and E. Greenberg, *A Treasury of Yiddish Stories* (New York, 1954), p. 230.

In Chapter IV, verse 4, of *Mishnah Aboth*: "Levitas of Jabneh said: Be exceeding lowly of spirit, for the hope of man is but the worm." Hermann Cohen quotes the Rambam's commentary to *Mishnah Aboth* to illustrate the virtue of humility. In addition, Cohen declared that this virtue distinguished Jewish ethics from Greek and post-Greek ethics. *The Commentary to Mishnah Aboth*, trans. Arthur David (New York, 1968), pp. 65–66: "On the ship were merchants and wealthy men. I was lying in my place and one of the men arose to urinate. I was insignificant and contemptible in his sight because in his sight I was very low, until he uncovered his nakedness and urinated on me. . . . As the Lord lives, my soul was not pained at his deed at all nor was my power aroused within me. Instead, I rejoiced greatly when I attained the limit where the contempt of that deficient man did not pain me. . . ." I would like to thank Prof. Rotenstreich for calling my attention to this commentary. See *R.d.V.*, p. 495.

Tugendweg zur Annaeherung an Gott.[72] This concluding remark of Cohen points to his attempt to read the history of man in terms of biblical faith; but even more, he has attested the biblical evaluation of life's meaning. In this humility there is a spark of greatness. The profound realization of our finiteness enhances man's moral and religious task, for alone in the depth of this finiteness lie Judaism's rejection of pantheism and sanctification of the moral deed.

Reflecting back on a work of Kant, *The Conflict of the Faculties* (1798), and to his characterization of the theologian who proves the existence of God by the fact that He has spoken in the Bible, it is hard to avoid the conclusion that Cohen—who now lets the Bible speak for his truths—has in many respects become the theologian in a Kantian sense.[73] The significance of this new direction in Cohen's thought becomes somewhat clear when we recall Kant's conclusion in the *Critique of Judgment*. If we thought a supreme purpose, an *Endzweck* for creation, we could think of no other than man *under* moral law but not *in accordance* with moral law.[74] In the *Ethik* man stood under the moral law. He, as a moral being, was the supreme purpose of creation; the ideal of virtue was the expression of the moral law, and the realization of *Sophrosyne* was the fullest delineation of this ideal. All reality was subsumed under this ideal. There could, however, be a divine purpose and the virtues would be the paths, *die Wegweiser*, to it, but faith and not philosophy would have to set this new purpose. The Bible could reveal a new purpose for creation, and this knowledge of God would be the object of man's highest love. It is this attempt by Cohen to bring forth and communicate a new purpose that constitutes the nature of the shift in his thinking. The prayer for a new heart and the contriteness of the spirit are the paths that indicate that the supreme human purpose is in reality a preparation only for a divine service. Justice, the virtue of the state, is now for Cohen transformed into a sign of the messianic age.[75]

72 *R.d.V.*, p. 496: "In dieser Weisheit vom Ursprung und vom Ende des Menschenleben gegruendet sich die Demut als eines der Fundamente der Seele, und demgemaess als das Fundament der Froemmigkeit."

73 "Eigentuemlichkeit der theologischen Fakultaet," *Der Streit der Fakultaeten* (Hamburg: Meiner Verlag, 1959), pp. 15–16: "Dass ein Gott sei, beweist der biblische Theolog daraus, dass er in der Bibel geredet hat. . . . Er wird es also als Glaubenssache auf ein gewisses Gefuehl der Goettlichkeit derselben . . . gruenden. . . ."

74 *K.d.U.*, p. 422: ". . . dass, wenn ueberal ein Endzweck, den die Vernunft a priori angeben muss, stattfinden soll, dieser kein anderer als der Mensch (ein jedes vernuenftigen Weltwesen) unter moralischen Gesetzen sein koenne. Note, Nicht der Mensch nach moralischen Gesetzen . . . naemlich dass es in der Gewalt eines Welturhebers stehe, zu machen, dass der Mensch den moralischen Gesetzen jederzeit sich angemessen verhalte. . . ."

75 *R.d.V.*, p. 497: "So wird die Gerechtigkeit zum Kennzeichen des messianischen Zeitalters. . . . Das Aufhoeren der Kriege ist das negative Kennzeichen des messianischen Zeitalters, das positive ist auch subjektiv im Lernen und in der Gewoehnung der Gerechtigkeit."

Justice is the second virtue Cohen considers. Its origin lies deep in Israel's history. The exodus from Egypt is to be remembered, for from this remembrance there is derived the strength of virtue. The slavery of Egypt is the source of that constantly renewed command against oppression and injustice.[76] For in God as the advocate of the orphan, the stranger, and the widow there emerges that close link which Cohen so often sought between religion and ethics. God must become king in Israel, but the realization of his kingdom depends upon the fulfillment of justice in the community. Israel under the Kingdom of God would be the way through which God would become king of all men.[77] In justice Israel prepares for the Kingdom of God.

Men must accept sufferings and bear them as the "sufferings of love." At the center of this reality lies the history of Israel's chosenness, her exile, and her redemption. This drama is eternally revealed in her monadic reality, i.e., the interplay of her historical existence and her eternity. It is the drama of the sufferings of love for the divine uniqueness and awareness that must embrace all men as it embraces the community of Israel. The redemption of Israel in love is symbolic of this redemption of all men. In Israel's sufferings Cohen understands the sufferings of all the afflicted; Israel suffers for the downtrodden and the scorned, but in her faith they are healed. As in the *Contempt of Religion*, the image of the suffering servant is always before Cohen. The history of Israel's exile and redemption has become Cohen's theodicy.[78] God has chosen Israel. He has revealed to her the falsity of polytheism and anthropomorphism; her reality contradicts these falsehoods in all their implication from the philosophical to the political and social.[79] Only in the faith of knowledge does the *monos* of monotheism slowly emerge, and with it begins the true history of religion and humanity. The justice now encompassed in theodicy explains Israel's sufferings of love as the "martyrdom of monotheism," *das Martyrium des Monotheismus*. It is in the *Shabbath*, the redemption from slavery

[76] *R.d.V.*, p. 499: "So ist die ganze Thora ein Andenken an die Befreiung aus der aegyptischen Sklaverei, welche als die Wiege des juedischen Volkes nicht beklagt, geschweige verdammt, sondern in Dankbarkeit gefeiert wird."

[77] *R.d.V.*, p. 498: "Auf der Gerechtigkeit beruht die juedische Theokratie . . . weil sonst Gott nicht Koenig sein koennte in Israel, nicht Koenig werden koennte in der Menschheit, in der ganzen Erde." The universalism for Cohen's thought is well illustrated in the chapter "Die Entdeckung des Menschen als des Mitmenschen," where he discussed the seven Noachidic obligations, their fulfillment, and the subsequent share in eternal life which they confer on all men. See Elie Benamozegh, *Israel et l'humanité* (Paris, 1961).

[78] *R.d.V.*, p. 502: "Diese Theodizie geht dem Propheten bei der Geschichte seines Volkes auf; mit ihr verklaert sich ihm das Leiden des Exils."

[79] *R.d.V.*, p. 502: "Die Erwaehlung zur Lehre des Einzigen Gottes ist zugleich die Erwaehlung zu dem stellvertretenden Leide fuer die Goetzendiener, wie fuer alle Voelker, die noch nicht zur Erkenntnis des einzigen Gottes ausgereift sind."

and labor, that the fulfillment of the divine creation takes place.[80] It is the goal of the "martyrdom of monotheism" to extend the significance of the Shabbath to all men and to all time, for in it a moment of messianic humanity is achieved and justice is learned by all men. Over and over again the moral substance of Cohen's religious faith is manifested and embodied in the ethical deductions which he knows must be and can be made from every true religious insight. Religion is a calling to bring about the truth of God, and because the historical Israel believes in the efficacy of that truth—although she is unaware at any particular moment of all its content—she makes her life and her work in accordance with that truth.[81] In Cohen the struggle for monotheism was at first a philosophic truth that permeated his systematic thought; now it is the truth of God and the source of his struggle against myth, polytheism, and anthropomorphism. It is from these struggles that the realization of the truth of God's incomparableness arises. The "martyrdom of monotheism" is the destiny upon which depends "the being or not being of the moral universe." The moral universe is at stake when we speak of monotheism; the fall into divination, into idolatry, threatens its very existence. The aloneness of Israel is analogous to the pureness of Cohen's philosophic methodology. The message of monotheism can only proceed from Israel's separateness; it can proceed from Israel as God's kingdom.[82] Aloneness and pureness are the corresponding realities that link Cohen the believer to Cohen the philosopher.

Cohen ends his discussion of the virtue of justice with the warning that the sufferings of Israel have no relation to punishment.[83] The yoke of the kingdom of God is not to be framed within movements of an Aeschylean drama, but the yoke of God is worn in love and faith; world history depends upon the courage of Israel. The word *Israel* is enhanced and broadened by Cohen to include the pious of the world, for would it not destroy the universal of the "martyrdom of monotheism" if it meant nothing more than Israel's self-glorification? "The election of Israel constitutes in no sense an exception. It is rather the symbolic confirmation of

[80] *R.d.V.*, p. 499: "Der Shabbat ist nicht sowohl des Menschen wegen da, sondern vornehmlich des Sklaven, des Arbeiters wegen. Und dieser Shabbat bezeichnet zugleich die Vollendung der goettlichen Weltschoepfung."

[81] *R.d.V.*, p. 503: "Das hoechste Glueck Israels sein geschichtlicher Beruf fuer den einzigen Gott, diese seine Bevorzugung, als welche der geschichtliche Beruf gedacht und gefuehlt werden muss, wenn er wirksam werden und bleiben soll, wird nunmehr durch die Stellvertretung des Leidens ausgeglichen."

[82] *R.d.V.*, p. 271: "Die Absonderung geht voran. Sie war die Vorbedingung schon fuer die Erhebung zum Monotheismus, geschweige fuer seine Erhaltung. Ferner aber darf das Unrecht nicht herrschen in Israel."

[83] *R.d.V.*, p. 503: "Die Gerechtigkeit vollendet sich nicht in der Strafe, aber allerdings in einem solchen Leiden, welches der Mensch ueber sich verhaengt erkennt im Berufs der Weltgeschichte, vom Joche des Gottesreiches, unter dem Bekenntnis des einzigen Gottes der Menschheit."

the love of God for the whole race of man . . . Israel being His peculiar possession . . . a model and . . . a symbol for the whole of mankind."[84]

The virtue of courage is characterized by Cohen as the triumph of humanity, *der Triumph des Menschentum.* In the *Ethik* courage was the virtue of Idealism; it was a virtue in behalf of a philosophical theory. Socrates suffered the martyrdom of philosophy; his courage served the demands of thought. Religiously Socrates remained true to the god of Asclapius, the healer, and if his accusers claimed that he introduced new gods, these, Cohen states, were only concepts derivative from his philosophic outlook.[85] Socratic courage is nothing less than the embodiment of the virtue of courage Cohen had posited for the work of culture. It was this virtue that gave us command over the sensuous inclinations; it was the courage to stand under the moral law and to act as if the moral law had taken form. "Courage is the capacity and resolved purpose to resist a strong but unjust opponent; and with regard to the opponent of the moral disposition within us, such courage is virtue."[86] Cohen in his *Ethik* had extended the definition of the "opponent" to all attempts to dissolve or to weaken the absolute requirement of his methodology resulting in a dilution of its rational purity. The courage to carry through his *idealism* he identified with the work of culture. In this context Socratic courage is the philosophic ideal. In contrast, the Jewish martyr is a hero for the God of Israel; not a God of theory, but the God of his faith, his Fathers, his history, and ultimately the God of all men.[87] Courage is the virtue of history; but no longer do we deal with the individual under moral law, free from all historical condition, but with the individual immersed in history and obligated to it, the individual within a holy history, meta-historical in dimension yet historical in development.[88] We can call it monadic history. The individual has been gathered into a people, and it is in this people that the individual achieves

[84] *R.d.V.*, p. 173: ". . . dass die Erwaehlung Israels keineswegs eine Ausnahme, sondern vielmehr die symbolische Bestaetigung bildet von der Liebe Gottes zu dem Menschengeschlecht . . . Israel Israel ist sein Eigentum . . . als Vorbild, als Symbol der Menschheit." This quotation was cited in translation by Hugo Bergman in "Israel and the Oikoumene," p. 62.

[85] *R.d.V.*, p. 507: "Er [Socrates] selbst opfert dem Asklepius einen Hahn. So erkennt er selbst den historischen Wert der vaeterlichen Gottheit an. Daher ist auch sein Martyrium nicht sowohl ein religioeses als ein theoretisches: das Selbstopfer des Philosophen."

[86] *M.d.S.*, p. 380: "Nun ist das Vermoegen und der ueberlegte Vorsatz, einem starken, aber ungerechten Gegner Widerstand zu tun, die Tapferkeit, und in Ansehung des Gegners der sittlichen Gesinnung in uns Tugend."

[87] *R.d.V.*, p. 507: "Der juedische Maertyrer dagegen ist ein Held fuer den einzigen Gott Israels, der night allein sein Gott, der Gott seiner Theorie sei es auch seines Glaubens ist, sondern zugleich der Gott seiner Vaeter, der Gott seiner Geschichte, der deshalb auch der Gott der Menschheit gedacht werden kann."

[88] *R.d.V.*, p. 507: "Die juedische Tapferkeit ist daher schlechthin eine Tugend der Geschichte, des geschichtlichen Menschen, nicht des Individualen."

his purpose. Here he must live according to the messianic purpose that the people, from the beginning, have chosen to serve. A decade earlier Cohen spoke to Herrmann of his faith in the historical meaning of Israel and at the same time wrote a neo-Kantian ethics in which Israel's exile and redemption, "her martyrdom for monotheism," played no role. Cohen now writes a philosophy of religion, a theodicy, in which the script of the moral universe is read in the "sufferings of love" that have become symbolic of Israel's history.

Human courage was put forth in behalf of a vast philosophic undertaking to unify the logic of pure knowledge with the purity of will and feeling. The virtue of courage served to assure this theoretical endeavor, the endeavor of man endowed with reason. But the Jew embodied a particular courage; he had to have that peculiar virtue of courage to assure the existence of the truth of the religious ideal of mankind.[89] Humanity is no longer a secular idea. Its origin is in messianism; it is the supreme consequence of monotheism.[90] The profound relationship between monotheism and a messianic humanity, the setting aside of all utopias and other eudaemonistic speculations, reveal that incomparable character of the Jewish hero, the servant of God, the hero of God who can live and defend his humanity only as a humble co-partner with God, *Bundesgenosse Gottes*. In this co-partnership lies the essence of correlation.[91]

It is in the "Sanctification of the Holy Name" that all the religious obligations find their objective expression. Only in so far as this "Sanctification" permeates all my activities can it become meaningful to speak of the unending approach to divine holiness.[92] Here Cohen can introduce a new aspect of Israel's martyrdom: the devotion of life to the "Sanctification of the Holy Name." There is implied in this a sanctification of the historical purpose of creation. The name of God is not yet *One*. This is the task of the historical future, this is the essence of hope, the theodicy that gives meaning to the "sufferings of love," for these sufferings can

[89] *R.d.V.*, p. 507: "Die menschliche Tapferkeit des Juden ist als geschichtliche Tugend die menschheitliche Tapferkeit, die Tapferkeit fuer die Wahrheit des religioesen Ideals der Menschheit."

[90] *R.d.V.*, p. 507: ". . . das die Menschheit, die allgemach zu einer ethischen Idee geworden ist, ihrem Ursprunge im Messianismus gemaess, eine religioese Idee ist, die hoechste, aber unfehlbare Konsequenz des messianischen Monotheismus."

[91] *R.d.V.*, p. 506: "Er [the hero] kann daher sein Menschtum nur leben und verteidigen als Bundesgenosse Gottes, als Knecht Gottes, und so auch als Held Gottes." Also, p. 129 (Cohen etches the ideal structure of correlation as eternal task): "Er sollte Heiliger werden koennen in dem Sinne, dass er das Menschenmass ueberfloege, dass er der Gottheit sich faktisch annaehern duerfte, waehrend diese Annaeherung, vielmehr die Durchfuehrung der Korrelation mit Gott nur seine ewige Aufgabe, nur sein ewiges Ziel bildet."

[92] *R.d.V.*, pp. 507–8: "Und indem ich des Inhalts dieses Gedankens von der Heiligkeit Gottes mich bemaechtige, vollziehe ich meine Selbstheiligung, die nichts anderes ist als die unendlich Annaeherung an die Heiligkeit Gottes."

have no tint of sadism; they are the witness to the future, the knowledge that on that day the name of God will be one.[93] The virtue of courage is the historical lot that the Jew takes upon himself, and it is upon this courage that the oneness of the Holy Name depends. The deepest and holiest thoughts of the human spirit are inseparably bound with the messianic future.[94] The danger inherent in all messianic thinking is the sacrifice of the present in behalf of the future. Cohen at the end of his *Ethik* in his discussion of *Sophrosyne* spoke of the present as the area of ultimate moral concern. The individual, in the concreteness of his reality, could not be set aside for futuristic speculations.[95] Although Cohen treats the virtues within the framework of Israel's world-historical odyssey, he stresses the concreteness of their moral necessitation. This necessitation is strengthened rather than weakened when their positive reality is transfigured by a meta-historical one, whose truth must always be justified in positive moral action.

The virtue of faithfulness, *Treue*, is no longer an individual excellence but the virtue of a people. The people are the guardian of the Tradition, and the obligation to teach and learn stems from what Cohen had called the archetype of all commands, the "Sanctification of the Holy Name."[96] Trust in human reason, in the unity of spirit and will, is the guarantor of their efficacy, while faithfulness to the Tradition is molded by its truth and the theodicy which it embodies. This virtue of faithfulness is the positive expression of Cohen's belief not only in the truth of redemptive history, but in the educative framework which has been the source of the continuation of the belief in this history. The work of culture required a faithfulness which Cohen could give as philosopher or as a believer in reason. The faithfulness that he gives as a Jew is to a concrete, positive, historical tradition that he believes incorporates the truth of God. From the first covenant with Abraham, which implied a covenant for all the future generations, to

[93] *R.d.V.*, p. 508: "Wie Gott einzig ist, so werde dereinst auch sein Name einzig sein. So hofft, so betet der Jude. Und wie er in jedem Individuum um dieses messianischen Zieles willen leidet, so wird er fuer diesen geschichtlichen Glauben zum Maertyrer, wenn er ihn unter Androhung des Todes verleugnen soll."

[94] *R.d.V.*, p. 508: ". . . jeder Jude die Tugend der Tapferkeit als sein geschichtliches Los auf sich nimmt, mit der ganzen Lebensfreudigkeit des Todesmutes . . . fuer den tiefsten und heiligsten Gedanken des menschlichen Geistes."

[95] *Ethik*, p. 635. See also the view of Rotenstreich, *Spirit and Man*, p. 185: "But practically we turn concrete human beings into means only and thus on behalf of freedom to be realized in the future, we uproot freedom as feature of living human reality." See the article of Hugo Bergman, "Die Hoffnung der Juden," in *Juden Christen Deutsche* (Stuttgart, 1961), pp. 249–57; also Ernst Bloch, *Tuebinger Einleitung II* (Frankfurt am Main, 1964), p. 176. Also Gershom Scholem's article, "Zum Verstaendnis der messianischen Idee im Judentum," in *Judaica*, p. 73.

[96] *R.d.V.*, p. 512: "Die Treue am Studium der Lehre hat den vornehmen Charakter der Volksseele nicht untergehen lassen unter den Bedrueckungen der Jahrtausende."

the faithfulness of Hermann Cohen, there has been one virtue that has maintained the historical bond, the virtue of faithfulness, without which all the other virtues lose their efficaciousness.[97] The virtue of faithfulness which Cohen now expresses is indeed in contrast with the virtue which he detailed in his *Ethik*. There is, however, never a loss of faithfulness to reason, to the ideal of reason, and to the work of culture; but the truth of monotheism and its historical and meta-historical dimensions necessitates a faithfulness not only equal to the philosophical, but superior to it. There seems to be little doubt that the philosophic principles with which Cohen developed his system are inseparable from the purity of monotheism and perhaps are derived from it while his religious thought is completely immersed in it. Faithfulness within the religious frame does not belong any longer to the conceptual language of philosophy; it is expressed in the language and style of prayer. Nothing is more illustrative of this than Cohen's article concerned with the lyrics of the Psalms, for he is well aware that the whole edifice of the philosophy of religion can remain in a purely conceptual undertaking, and religion does not become a lived experience.[98] It is only in the language of faithfulness, in prayer, that this concrete experience of the believer comes alive. The abstractness of Cohen's speculations dissolves in the language of prayer, for it is in this language that the correlation between man and God becomes positive and meaningful; in it man cleanses himself before the Divine. Prayer is the verbal organ of Messianism. The virtue of faithfulness discovers its strength in prayer; all other styles and languages fail when the strength to bear this faithfulness is in question. So central is prayer that in a concise way the *Malhuyot*, the *Zihronot* and *Shoferot* of the New Year Musaf service, embodies the religious essence of Cohen's belief. The majesty of the divine sovereignty, the expression of the moral world order, *die sittliche Weltordnung*; the divine remembrance, the world standing open before God who "rememberest from eternity all forgotten things"; the hope in the future redemption when God shall be a "shield" over Israel; it is this triadic reality that reveals the *mysterium tremendum* of Cohen's moral and religious world. The language of this world is spoken in prayer.

[97] *R.d.V.*, p. 514: "Was waere am letzten Ende aller Erfolg der Gerechtigkeit und nicht minder auch aller Tapferkeit, wenn beide absolute Tugenden nicht auf den Beistand rechnen koennten, die ihnen von dieser Tugend zweiten Grades sicher ist. Mehr noch, als die Bescheidenheit die Wahrhaftigkeit unterstuetzt, werden die Gerechtigkeit und die Tapferkeit von der Treue geradezu begleitet."

[98] "Die Lyrik der Psalmen" (1914). Also *R.d.V.*, p. 463: "So ist das Gebet die eigentliche Sprache der Religion. Und alles Denken dieser Sprache, von Gott und vom Menschen, alles Denken dieser Korrelation bliebe Theorie, wenn nicht das Gebet die Sprachhandlung wuerde, in welcher der Wille lebendig wird an allen Mitteln des Denkens." Also, ibid., p. 513: "Zu dieser Erhaltung, Staerkung, Laeuterung, Veredelung und Erhoehung der Treue sollen die Benediktionen des Gebetes die Anleitung geben."

The crown of the virtues is peace, *Friede*. So basic is this virtue that, according to Aggadic tradition, peace is one of God's names.[99] Peace is the ideal of messianic thought. In Kantian language it would be *das Ding an sich*, for it can only be represented by pure reason, *das, was nur durch reine Vernunft dargestellt werden kann*,[100] and yet the practical–moral reason in us requires that we work for those conditions that would make its establishment a reality. Cohen, however, goes beyond the practical–moral command of reason, "There shall be no war," and finds the source of peace in God, the oneness and incomparableness of his essence. "The chastisement for our welfare *Shalom* was upon him" (Isa 53:5). The suffering of the Messiah becomes a means for the realization of this peace. Philosophic truths are transformed into religious truths, and the ideas of reason are transfigured into the living religious imagery of Israel's symbolic meaning and significance as means for a universal moral redemption. Peace is the purpose of this redemptive struggle; it is more embracing and total than the Greek virtue of *Sophrosyne*, which Cohen had identified with *Humanitaet*. It encompasses the messianic reconciliation of all creation.[101]

Peace is the highest human achievement, an expression of the greatest human power. It can be called the ideal. *Sophrosyne* is the archetype of the virtues, it presupposes a prudential "sight," it is the culminating intellectual virtue. Peace requires an acceptance of the universal divine kingship, of a kingdom of faith and of an eternal faithful people. It is a kingdom in which eudaemonism and sophism have been negated. Its values lie beyond the worldly material attractions; its truths have only begun to be revealed in their historical journey. The accompanied sufferings are not unknown elements, and at moments of great moral heights they are transfigured into "sufferings of love."[102] Though the messianic age might be delayed for thousands of years, there was an assurance that in the truth of the divine providence the day would surely come. It was this reconciliation with the coming of the messianic age that made the path to peace a holy one, but it was also a path that could avoid the despair that clustered around this messianic peace and drove men to reject the world.[103] Belief is not adequate,

[99] A. Marmorstein, *The Old Rabbinic Doctrine of God*, I, *The Names and Attributes of God* (London, 1927), 104–5. Cf. G. Scholem, *Jewish Gnosticism, Merkabah Mysticism and Talmudic Tradition* (New York, 1965), p. 134, n. 76, 1. 30. *R.d.V.*, p. 517: "Gott ist der Friede . . . Gott als Zweck ist gleichbedeutend mit Gott als Frieden."

[100] *M.d.S.*, p. 371. A clear and precise definition of the *Ding an sich*.

[101] *R.d.V.*, p. 516: "Denn der Friede ist das Wahrzeichen des messianischen Zeitalters, und zwar nicht nur als Gegensatz zum Kriege, der verschwinden wird, sondern auch positiv, insofern er den Inbegriff aller Sittlichkeit bildet."

[102] *R.d.V.*, p. 518: ". . . denn sie betrifft die Anerkennung der goettlichen Vorsehung und Weltregierung. Vor der Zufriedenheit zerschellen alle Anstuerme des Eudaemonismus, alle Zweifel selbst, welche das tiefste Seelenleid erregen koennten."

[103] *R.d.V.*, p. 519: "Soll nun aber aus solcher Seelenstimmung nicht der Quietismus entstehen, der die Mystik beguenstigt und die Asketik, die Weltflucht und die Enthaltung von

for without knowledge true peace is unattainable. The way that God shows cannot be known by belief alone, and the command to do justice, for righteousness and loving kindness, is not fulfilled without study and learning.[104] The knowledge of God is the love of God; from His Being and attributes flow those commandments for justice and righteousness upon which the moral universe depends.[105] The freedom from injustice prepares for the messianic age, an age in which the knowledge of God will be the concern of man. Maimonides states: "Ce n'est pas par la domination d'Israel sur les autres nations que la fin des temps sera marquées, mais par l'affranchissement de l'humanité de toutes les servitudes qui l'empêchent se donner entièrement à la tâche de connaître Dieu."[106] The messianic calling of the Jew stands in the most intimate relationship with the knowledge of the Torah and its extension to all mankind. Although Cohen had clearly separated philosophy from religion in all his previous works, it appears that in this final work the division vanishes, for in the messianic age the goals of philosophy and religion are united. The universal domination of knowledge is necessarily linked and bound to the messianic destiny of mankind. If Israel is the mediator in this destiny, there is joy in this knowledge and a spiritual peace that reflects the relationship of truth.[107]

Cohen had struggled all his life against philosophies of feeling, pessimism, and skepticism; he knew of their political effects for all his fellow Jews. The messianism of the Torah gave to Israel the uniqueness of her lot, a universalism that struggled against hate and atavism. In hate lie the roots of perversity; this Cohen had already noted in the *Ethik* and had observed that the rawness of hate was usually and attractively disguised by sophisticated national and religious motives.[108] *Humanitaet*

---

den buergerlichen Pflichten des Staatsleben, muss diese Zufriedenheit gewappnet sein mit derjenigen Kulturkraft, welche allein die Erkenntnis bildet."

[104] *R.d.V.*, p. 519: "Nicht der Glaube schlechtin darf den Menschen befriedigen . . . nicht der Glaube ohne Erkenntnis begruendet den wahren Seelenfrieden, die wahrhafte religioese Zufriedenheit mit dem Geschicke, sondern die Vernunft, die Erkenntnis ist der Wurzelboden. . . ."

[105] *R.d.V.*, p. 519. Typical of Cohen's religious rationalism is his conviction that wisdom rests on learning: *Weisheit beruht auf Gelehrsamkeit*. Cohen was proud that his thought continued the tradition of Maimonides, and it gave him great comfort to be able to say about this that the Rambam would be pleased. See his article "Charakteristik der Ethik Maimonis," *J.S.*, vol. III (1908), originally published in *Moses ben Maimon: Sein Leben, seine Werke und sein Einfluss* (Leipzig, 1908).

[106] G. Vajda, *Introduction à la pensée juive du moyen âge* (Paris, 1947), p. 143n. The citation is from the end of Maimonides' Code (Hilkot Melakim, XII, 4).

[107] *R.d.V.*, p. 520: "Seine Zufriedenheit wurzelt in seinem messianischen Berufe, der die Erkenntnis der Thora und die Pflicht ihrer Verbreitung in der geschichtlichen Welt zur Voraussetzung at hat. . . . Diese Freude an der Thora ist der Frieden der Seele, die Feste der Zufriedenheit."

[108] *Ethik*, p. 633: "Der Hass und die Grausamkeit decken ja selten nur die Wurzeln der Perversitaet auf, aus denen sie hervortreiben; sie decken und schmuecken sich mit hohen

was the weapon that could hopefully negate these cultural perversities.[109] But *Humanitaet* assumes a world that arises from reason in a practical–moral sense, a noumenal world centered in man as subject of morality. Cohen adds to the ethical speculation biblical texts whose validity, although not contrary to ethics, nevertheless is grounded in religious faith. As an example he cites "Thou shalt not hate thy brother in thy heart" (Lev 19:17); these are texts that man must know and believe, for in accordance with them he must act. The world is created through correlation; its moral reality should become concomitant with the Being of the Creator. Man's moral activity redeems a creation that is yet unaware of its truth and the source of its reality. The meaning of creation and revelation is unfolded in the contrast and mutuality that fills correlation.[110] Correlation on a cosmic scale embraces symbolically a messianic kingdom that ties through love and justice the uniqueness of God to the oneness of mankind. The highest endeavor of reason has become the clarification of the divine purpose of creation, the knowledge of God.

Hate is derisive. It tears man from man and nation from nation; it is vanity. *Aller Hass ist umsonst*. Hate is moral violence. It diminishes and finally destroys the subject of morality, moral man; it is the death of the person. I cannot even suppose that I hate another, for the supposition is violence and with it crumble the human dialogue, the world; terror is its consequence.[111] The depth of Cohen's insight into the problem of hate is his firm dismissal of attempts to ascribe even false reason to hate, when the essence of hate is, in fact, that it has no ground. In this lies its terror. As long as the possibility of hate exists, be it my own or that of another, there can be no peace.[112] Cohen had already made the linkage between hate, cruelty, and sexual perversity. Their embodiment in a political idealogy he did not yet envision; the dehumanization expressed in disgust, *Ekel*, he had already assumed in a hate that was *grundlos und eitel*. Kant had already shown how deep this dehuminization went when he pointed to the utter inability of beautiful art to represent that which excited disgust:

Motiven, in deren Dienst sie staenden."

[109] *Ethik*, p. 633: "Die Humanitaet allein vermag alle jene Vorgaenge der Kultur unwegsam zu machen."

[110] *R.d.V.*, p. 108: "Was waere damit gewonnen, wenn ich die Geheimnisse der Schoepfung und der Offenbarung durchringen koennte? Wuerde ich dadurch das einzige Sein Gottes besser verstehen, als ich es durch die Korrelation zu verstehen habe?" See p. 212: "Und da die Schoepfung selbst auch nur eine Form dur Korrelation ist, so ist die Selbstheiligung die notwendige Folge dieser Schoepfung der Heiligkeit Gottes."

[111] *R.d.V.*, p. 522: "Ich bestreite . . . dass ich einen Feind habe, dass ich einen Mensch hassen koennte. Was ist der Hass? Ich bestreite seine Moeglichkeit. Es ist ein eitles Wort, das einen solchen Begriff bezeichnen will."

[112] *R.d.V.*, p. 522: "Solange der Hass mich bedroht, der fremde wie der eigene, so lange kann ich mich keines Friedens getroesten und keiner echten Zufriedenheit."

> The Furies, diseases, the devastations of war may even regarded as calamitous be described as very beautiful, as they are represented in a picture. There is only one kind of ugliness [*Haesslichkeit*] which cannot be represented in accordance with nature without destroying all aesthetical satisfaction . . . that which excites disgust [*Ekel*].[113]

Hate terrorizes the human, morally and aesthetically. It shows neither contrast nor contradictions that might be gathered into new harmonies, but it destroys the human substance and reduces man to bestiality. Hate penetrates only where the spirit weakens, hope fades, and the practical-moral values and beliefs decline.[114]

Closely related to the problem of hate is that of pessimism. Cohen radically opposes all attempts to ascribe to evil a positive power; in such mystical schemes where the power of the evil and the power of the good are in eternal conflict, the moral substance of monotheism is wrecked.[115] More deeply moral than any other belief of monotheism is that which declares that before God, man is made innocent, *Gott macht unschuldig*. The *Shegaga*, unintentional sin, is the limit of man's fault. Man's guilt cannot but be momentary. To ascribe to man an evil character cannot but be an excuse to lessen or diminish the moral and religious task placed upon him.[116] The purification of man takes place before God. It is the trust in Him, in His truth, that is the ground of the new truth, the new beginning, and the new hope. Every man can assume the task of holiness; it was given to him as an eternal obligation by a God that is Holy. Eternal Israel is that pure demand of holiness that characterizes her universal significance for all mankind. It is in her midst that God is hallowed.

In contrast to the symbol of eternal Israel, man must be ever seeking purification, a new heart; this is the purification before God that renews the strength for moral redemption.

> No man purifies you; and no man who is at the same time supposed to be God. No son of God shall purify you, but your Father only. And also you shall not purify yourselves before any other mediating being. Only when God, simply and solely, is the unique and single aim of your purification, only then can purification be achieved.[117]

[113] *K.d.U.*, p. 189: "Die Furien, Krankheiten, Verwuestung des Krieges koennen, als Schaedlichkeiten sehr schoen beschrieben, ja sogar im Gemaelde vorgestellt werden; nur eine Art Haesslichkeit kann nicht der Natur gemaess vorgestellt werden, ohne alles aesthetische Wohlgefallen . . . zugrunde zu richten: naemlich diejenige, welche Ekel erweckt" (trans. Bernard, p. 155).

[114] *R.d.V.*, p. 524: "Und so wahr Geist, Gottes Geist in dem Herzen des Menschen lebt, so ist es nicht Hass, der seine Tatkraft bezwingt."

[115] *R.d.V.*, p. 524: ". . . denn er [pessimismus] ist nicht eine Erkenntnis der Vernunft, sondern eine Eingebung der Mystik. Er widerspricht der Guete und der Vorsehung Gottes."

[116] *R.d.V.*, p. 524. See the chapter "The Day of Atonement," particularly p. 260.

[117] *R.d.V.*, p. 261: "Kein Mensch reinigt euch, und auch kein Mensch, der zugleich ein

Religion became a sublime defiance of all attempts to reduce man to the woes of his positive condition, to sufferings and to his despair; it is in the very midst of these realities that the truth of God is proclaimed in faithfulness.[118] The symbol of suffering Israel gives lie to pessimism, for it is the eternal embodiment of the symbol of redemption. Philosophies of pessimism had no place in Judaism, ethics, and Messianism. In the *Ethik* Cohen pointed to the danger of these philosophies, both for the history of rational thought and for the historic mission of monotheism. He never wavered in his belief that his own philosophy had stood in the tradition of Plato, Maimonides, Leibniz, and Kant, and that moral optimism is coterminous with a belief in the rationality of man. Cohen philosophized from philosophic to religious tradition; the eternal movement and development of thought unfolded ever-new dimensions of reason, while in Israel's Messianism lay the monotheistic redemption of mankind; the two are ultimately one. Totality in philosophy is the self-consciousness of purity; monotheism is the truth of God in his oneness and uniqueness, a truth of unique purity. Philosophy and religion are joined in the oneness of reason and the uniqueness of God. They effect a similar universal task in knowledge and ethics.

Peace is a feeling that comes over us when we become aware that someone has done good. We must assume a susceptibility and a feeling for the moral and the sublime. There is a joy in this feeling and a desire and a thirst for its continuance, but joy is even more an expression of our receptivity—not only for the moral, but for each act of repentance that helps unlock the "Holy of Holies."[119] Although joy seems to have yielded to suffering in Cohen's theodicy, joy in faith was one of the deepest revelations of the truth of his belief and perhaps of all belief both religious and philosophical. Joy emanates from within the religious; it embraces peace as the supreme virtue, the culminating point of justice and courage, and proclaims its messianic reality. The feeling of joy is the limit of suffering, the obstacle that opposes its fall into sadism and pessimism. Joy is the sign,

---

Gott sein soll. Kein Sohn Gottes soll euch reinigen, sondern eurer Vater allein. Und auch vor keinem anderen Mittelwesen sollt ihr euch reinigen, sondern nur wenn Gott der einzige und alleinige Zielpunkt eurer Selbstreinigung ist, nur dann kann sie vollbracht werden" (trans. Simon Kaplan, part II).

[118] *R.d.V.*, p. 264: "Was der Mensch schlecht nennt, weil es ihm wehetut, das ist nicht in Wahrheit schlecht, sondern es geschieht zu seinem Guten. Das Leiden ist die Strafe, welche der Mensch unabtraeglich vor sich selbst, fuer sich selbst fordert."

[119] *R.d.V.*, p. 526: "Der Friede kommt ueber mich und beseeligt mich, wenn ich auch nur von einer erdichteten Handlung der Guete, von einem Menschen ausgefuehrt, hoere. . . . Was ginge mich die Maer von einer guten Handlung an, wenn mein Bewusstsein nicht an ihr Freude empfaende und nach ihr lechzte?" Kant said that to feel the sublime the mind must be cultivated for ideas. *K.d.U.*, p. 110: "Die Stimmung des Gemuets zum Gefuehl des Erhabenen erfordert eine Empfaenglichkeit desselben fuer Ideen. . . ." Joy must assume a religious commitment; it follows from it.

Wahrzeichen, of peace, but even more it is a cry of its strength and power.[120] In the *Ethik* the representation of the virtue of *Humanitaet* gave rise to a sense of moral power through which man feels himself superior to nature and becomes aware of the sublimity of his moral destiny. Cohen in the last pages of his *Ethik* could declare that this feeling is all, *Gefuehl ist alles*. Joy, on the other hand, is our awareness not so much of our moral destiny as it is a foreshadowing of the divine peace that is reflected in the reconciliation between both God and man, and man and man.[121] This peace, however,

> need not have its only meaning as the final link in the development of mankind, but it can and does take place at each moment in the historical development. Thus in the entire history of Israel we can detect the uninterrupted connection that exists between suffering and redemption. Redemption need not be postponed to the end of days; rather, it clings to every moment of suffering, and constitutes in each moment of suffering a moment of redemption.[122]

The longing for reconciliation, for the good in an indifferent world, is man's search for peace. Joy is symbolic of this messianic peace. It regains for man the equality lost in class distinction, in poverty, and it is in this peace that man can reconcile himself with himself as a moral person.

The joy of the religious celebrations reveals and expresses those moments of eternity that fill our longing for the knowledge of God and join all men as seekers of the same end.[123] With pointed concern and purpose, Cohen slips in the remark that these celebrations, and the joy attached to them, can in no way be related to the dionysian or bacchanalian with their orgiastic fascination with intoxication and ecstacy.[124] Cohen was always aware of the threat to his religious and moral position that was real in these romantic excesses, and in the philosophers who glorified them and built ethical systems upon them. He viewed the joy that was imbedded in the

[120] *R.d.V.*, p. 527: "Diese Freude ist ein Beweis fuer die Lebenskraft des Friedens."

[121] *R.d.V.*, p. 526: "Diese Versoehnlichkeit des Frieden . . . welche die Versoehnung des Menschen mit Gott bildet, welche aber zur Voraussetzung hat die Versoehnung zwischen Mensch und Mensch, und welche ihr Endergebnis hat in der Versoehung des Menschen mit sich selbst."

[122] *R.d.V.*, p. 274: "So koennen wir auch in der gesammten Geschichte Israels die ununterbrochene Verbindung erkennen, die zwischen dem Leiden und der Erloesung besteht. Die Erloesung braucht gar nicht hinausgeschoben zu werden aur das Ende der Tage, sondern sie haftet schon an jedem Moment des Leidens, und sie bildet an jedem Momente des Leidens einen Moment der Erloesung" (trans. Kaplan, part III).

[123] *R.d.V.*, p. 528: "Die Freude soll den Armen mit dir selbst verbinden. Du dollst dich freuen mit dem Armen. Und auch der Arme soll sich frauen mit dir. . . . Das Fest verloere seinen Sinn und Wert, wenn es nicht fuer diese wenigen Tage wenigstens die Freude aufzupflanzen vermoechte im Herzen des feiernden Menschen."

[124] *R.d.V.*, p. 528: "Diese Freude ist keine dionysische, keine bacchantische Lustfreude."

festivals, e.g., the Passover as the joy in the freedom from slavery, the formation of God's people, and their symbolic representation as a kingdom of priests.[125] The joy in the giving of the Torah, a joy in the law, *Gesetzesfreude*, this was the true moral and religious feeling that accompanied those monumental events in human history that accounted for the being or nonbeing of moral man and universe. Cohen could celebrate them and feel their overpowering sublimity. His ethics had prepared him for the religious in the fullness of its meaning. It would be difficult to imagine the vast impact that the religious would have made upon him if he had not been the author of *Ethik*. Religion came as a fulfillment, having already been preprared in the religiosity of his philosophy. The depth of his moral commitment and his passion for the ideal of humanity hover closely to the religious. The Jewish attachment to Messianism in all its ethical implications seems to have determined Cohen to bring together the best of both worlds.

If Judaism had given to mankind only the *Shabbath* it would have brought the most significant symbol of peace and joy.[126] Abysmal is the separation between the joy of the bacchanalia and the joy of the *Shabbath*; the separation penetrated deeply, for its consequences brought two worlds into existence, unbridgeable in their political, social, and economic realities. The joy and peace of the *Shabbath* arise from the contemplation of the fulfillment of creation, of the end of injustice, and of the monotheistic mission that will someday spread to all men and reconcile the truth of God with his creation.[127] The *Shabbath* is a moment of eternity that breaks forth into the profane. It is at the same time a noumenal reality only given in faith. It hovers over existence and proclaims its inadequacy and limitedness, its subjectivity and arbitrariness. This Cohen profoundly experienced in the reality of the *Shabbath*.[128] The messianic dimension of the *Shabbath* is analogous to Kant's realm of ends, *ein Reich der Zwecke*, but the latter is only an ideal and requires a *new being* who is without need and whose power is adequate to his will. That no such being is or can be without God's grace Kant never fails to assure us, and since Kant did not believe in the efficacy of this grace, the ideal

[125] *R.d.V.*, p. 528: "Ist es eine illusorische Freude, welche das Fest der Freiheit aufrichtet, der Befreiung aus dem Sklavenjoche, und der Berufung zum Volk Gottes und zum Reich von Priestern?"

[126] *R.d.V.*, p. 528: "Haette das Judentum nur den Shabbat der Welt gebracht, so waere es schon dadurch ausgewiesen als Freudenbringer und Friedensstifter in der Menschheit."

[127] *R.d.V.*, p. 183: "Und im Shabbat hat allerdings das Gesetz in Gemaessheit mit dem einzigen Gotte, der die Menschen liebt, das Jedentum, wie die Juden am Leben erhalten; beide in der Mission, den Monotheismus ueber die Erde zu verbreiten, seinen Sinn und Geist immer mehr zu vertiefen und ihm gemaess der wahre Menschenliebe unter den Voelkern der Welt zu begruenden."

[128] *R.d.V.*, p. 183: "Alle Muehsal aber des taeglichen Lebens warf der Gettojude von sich, wenn die Sattableuchter entzuendet wurden. Alle Schmach wurde abgeschuettelt."

remained mere ideal.[129] The *Shabbath* did not demand a new being for its realization; it belonged to and was experienced by the Jew not only in joy and peace, but it brought concrete moral obligations and anticipated a future whose messianic reality was not in doubt.[130] In correlation there is assumed the moral and religious adequacy of man; the world of correlation is rooted in that cosmic dialogue between God and Israel from which the moral emerges as task and obligation. For, as Israel is moved by her God, she reveals to man the eternal mission of monotheism: to transform through knowledge and justice the incompleteness of creation into messianic humanity.

The deep separation—the fallen world of man and the pure world of grace and redeemed man—has always dominated Christian thought and is clear in Kant. The subsequent pessimism is reflected in Kant's *Anthropology* and the *Metaphysics of Morals* when he speaks of man's nature and the ideal. His failure to believe in the actualization of the ideal reveals a moral dualism analogous to a religious one. Cohen, on the other hand, reflects that strong belief in man's capacity to sanctify both body and soul, to refuse all dualism that can threaten the moral obligation, and all pessimism that negates it. The correlation between Israel and God is a reality which enlarges and enhances the moral task, for Cohen believed that this moral task borne collectively by Israel would bring a new future and a new hope. In Israel the division between the holy and the profane, between the material and the spiritual, was healed, and it is for this reason that Cohen said that with the history of Judaism the history of religion has just begun. The history of Judaism has made only faint beginnings. Her monotheism has not yet transformed the world; its revolutionary nature is still to be experienced. Peace, that ultimate reconciliation of creation, is the Messiah; it is Israel's message and her martyrdom.[131] In her religious celebrations moments of this peace are enjoyed; there is a freedom from the anxiety of self-preservation, and the individual can live that reconciliation that is the essence of religion. To be yoked to the Law is to be yoked to the Kingdom of God; this is

[129] *Grundlegung zur Metaphysik der Sitten*, ed. Weischedel, IV, 67: ". . . wenn es ein voellig unabhaengiges Wesen, ohne Beduerfnis und Einschraekung seines dem Willen adequaten Vermoegens ist. . . ."

[130] *R.d.V.*, p. 529: "Die Welteroberung, welche dem Shabbat gelungen ist, kann die Hoffnung, die Zuversicht nicht sinken lassen, dass diese Freude kein leerer Wahn sei, und dass der Friede, der in dieser Freude ausstrahlt, eine Grundkraft des Menschengeschlechts sei und bleiben werde."

[131] *R.d.V.*, p. 529: "Der Friede als der Zweck des Menschen ist der Messias, der die Menschen und die Voelker von allem Zwiespalt befreit, den Zwiespalt im Menschen selbst schlichtet und endlich die Versoehnung fuer den Menschen erwirkt mit seinem Gotte."

the symbol of peace for all people.[132] The Law and its symbolic form as God's kingdom are the driving force of Cohen's Judaism. Israel announced the kingdom of God. This was the truth that she embodied; it was her "imperial message." The Kingdom was peace. It was the ultimate and supreme consequence of correlation; in the camp of Israel the "martyrs of monotheism" bring to dwell the divine. In the actuality of faith the finite gathers in moments of the infinite. In Cohen there lived that vision and imagery, those myths and symbols that made it possible to see in the people of God this actualization of the messianic hope for redemption. In every instant of the present a moment of reconciliation between creation and Creator is occurring through the mediation of Israel. Peace is the summary of all values; it is the end of the road traveled by the virtues. In peace they have their supreme end. The total human enterprise is meaningful when the end, *Endzweck*, is peace.[133]

Kant's pietism would have him say: "I will that there be a God, that my existence in this world be also an existence in a pure world of the understanding outside the system of natural connection, and finally that my duration be endless."[134] Kant was also certain that the conflict with Satan never ceased to fill man's soul. Luther had reduced the geography of the combat for man's soul to each individual. The Platonism and Realism of the Roman Church were reduced to Ockhamite limitations. In Cohen the vast Platonic world returns, but now it is transformed and redefined in Judaic terms. If it could be said that at a certain period in Cohen's thought Kant had found an interpreter or that Cohen's philosophy meant "a return to Kant," it finally could be said that in Cohen not only the Kantian ethic, but the metaphysics of Plato and Leibniz were ultimately vindicated.[135] In fact, the vast drama of suffering and messianism etched in the *Religion of Reason* is a theodicy whose moral–religious dimension and significance incorporate the insights and values that Cohen had identified, on the one hand, with a history of reason that had begun with Plato and ended with Kant, and on the other, with a monotheistic truth that lies at the beginning of all reality and is at the same time its redemption and transfiguration. To philosophize had become a religious act, and it is apparent that Cohen

[132] *R.d.V.*, p. 531: "Das Joch des Gesetzes war ihm [for the Jew] das Joch des Gottesreiches, und das Reich Gottes ist das Reich des Friedens fuer alle Voelker der ewigen Menschheit."

[133] *R.d.V.*, p. 531: "Aller Sinn, aller Wert des Lebens liegt im Frieden. . . . Der Friede ist die Krone des Lebens."

[134] *Kritik der Praktischen Vernunft*, ed. Weischedel, IV, 777–78: ". . . ich will, dass ein Gott, dass mein Dasein in dieser Welt, auch ausser der Naturverknuepfung, noch ein Dasein in einer reinen Verstandeswelt, endlich aus dass meine Dauer endlos sei. . . ." Trans. L. W. Beck, *Critique of Practical Reason* (Chicago, 1950), p. 245.

[135] See, in particular, Leibniz, "*Causa Dei* (A Vindication of God's Justice)", published as an appendix to the *Théodicée* (1710), par. 46 in *Monadology and Other Philosophical Essays*, trans. Paul Schrecker and Mary Schrecker (Indianapolis, 1965).

believed he had found a reconciliation both on the level of thought and in the truth of Israel. Philosophy and religion could be joined in the love and knowledge of God.

The final problem that Cohen considered was death. Although death has puzzled many men and some have asked for eternal life, as Gorky tells of Tolstoy's request, for Cohen death was not an end, a finale, but a new beginning.[136] In death the link is forged to the generations that began with the Fathers, forged to the eternity that is Israel, while at the same moment the future is called to remember the truth that is at the beginning.[137] It is the truth that is the beginning that has been the search of philosophy and is the faith of religion. The sciences build on what has been, only to seek new solutions; the past for science is perhaps less vital.[138] Death is a religious problem; it is the moment of reconciliation. There is no elaborate doctrine of Hell and punishment, but the hope that the soul will join the Fathers, become part of a servanthood that is co-extensive with human history.[139] In their faith they were already part of the days of the Messiah, for these days do not change nature. There is no thaumaturgy; they are the moments of trust that proclaim: "May He establish His Kingdom."[140] Cohen had rejected evil as an intrinsic element of creation. Death for him also did not exist. Israel is eternal; man's existence is only a moment in Israel's eternal history to which each Jew finitely and infinitely belongs. It was this reconciliation between the temporal and the eternal that Cohen called peace. Israel was for mankind a symbol of that messianic peace that redeems both evil and death.[141] Each Jew has an historical and meta-historical destiny;

[136] Maxim Gorky, *Reminiscences of Tolstoy, Chekhov and Andreyev* (New York, 1959). Why should not nature make an exception to her law, give to one man physical immortality? Cohen differently: "Der Tod ist nicht das Ende, aber ein Abschluss, ein neuer Anfang." *R.d.V.*, p. 531.

[137] *R.d.V.*, p. 531: "Daher bekundet sich sein Gedaechtnis fuer die Ueberlebenden in dem unvergaenglichen Gefuehl der Dankbarkeit und der aus ihr fliessenden Mahnung zur Liebespflicht und zum Verharren im Gehorsam, wie die Vorfahren ihn befolgt haben."

[138] S. H. Bergman, "Schelling on the Source of Eternal Truths," *Proceedings of the Israel Academy of Sciences and Humanities*, vol. II, No. 2 (Jerusalem, 1964): "The movement that constitutes the progress of philosophy differs, for good or ill, from that of the other disciplines in that it does not proceed from problem to problem but attempts to answer the same questions that haunted it at the beginning" (p. 17).

[139] *R.d.V.*, p. 532: "Wir feiern das Andenken unserer Toten in der frommen Hoffnung, dass ihre Seelen vereinigt werden mit den Seelen unserer Erzvaeter und Erzmuetter."

[140] *R.d.V.*, p. 532: ". . . so stirbt auch heute noch jeder Jude in der Hoffnung dieses geschichtlichen Fortlebens in dieser Vereinigung mit den Ahnherren seines Geschlechtes. So ist der Tod ein geschichtliches Fortleben. Und in diesem Fortleben waltet und herrscht der Friede, der allen Erdenkampf besiegt hat." "The historical continuity in no way diminishes the individual anguish which death induces, but it fills with awe and *fascinosum* the eternal bond between God and Israel."

[141] *R.d.V.*, p. 532-33: "Alles Zeitliche fuehrt zur Ewigkeit, wenn es den richtigen Weg geht. Und dieser rechte Weg, ist der des Friedens. Der Friede ist die Tugend der Ewigkeit."

his earthly death is transfigured into the eternal life of Israel. The grave is "the house of eternity." There is no death in Israel; all reality, historical and meta-historical, is subsumed in monotheism. The prayers, the festivals, the Law are forms of redemption and "Sanctification of the Holy Name" in which the creation is regained for the messianic humanity and the peace that is its truth. The moral universe is a consequence of the divine incomparableness; in Israel's divine odyssey the way is found to the days of the Messiah, that messianic peace which is the goal of all the virtues that Cohen had declared to be signs and paths to this peace.[142] The great struggle to reveal this truth of monotheism is thus the supreme religious and philosophical task, for upon this eternal verity of verities depends not only the moral universe, but the ultimate realization of that spirit which God implanted in man and which in correlation is known as the Holy Spirit, the spirit by which man takes his task to become holy from the Holiness that is his God.[143]

[142] *R.d.V.*, p. 533. Cohen's concluding words appear to indicate that intimate relationship between the historical and the eternal and perhaps their inseparability. Monotheism is truth; creation and revelation are meaningful only in terms of this truth. "Der Friede ist das Wahrzeichen der Ewigkeit und ebenso die Losung des menschlichen Lebens in seinem individuellen Verhalten, wie in der Ewigkeit seines geschichtlichen Berufes." I believe that a careful reading of Leibniz's monodology will show close parallels to Cohen's final metaphysics. See Leibniz, *Monodology*, ed. Schrecker, p. 154, e.g., par. 43 among others.

[143] *J.S.*, III, 189: "Ebenso ist jeder Mensch auch heilig; an jeden ist die Aufgabe der Heiligkeit ergangen, und durch jeden Menschen will Gott geheiligt werden." Also *R.d.V.*, p. 128: "Der heilige Geist wird im Menschen lebendig, insofern dieser sich heiligt. Und in dieser Selbstheiligung vollzieht er die Heiligung Gottes. Denn was sollte sonst die Heiligkeit bei Gott bedeuten, wenn sie nicht das Urbild waere fuer die Handlung des Menschen?"

Chapter IV

IMPLICATIONS OF COHEN'S ATTEMPT TO RELATE JUDAISM TO ETHICS

Hermann Cohen believed that the spread of the ideal of monotheism, messianic humanity, and peace depended upon the truth of Judaism. Kant had previously written in *Der Streit der Fakultaeten* that "Die Euthanasie des Judentums ist die reine moralische Religion . . ." (Weischedel, VI, 321), and only with the death of Judaism could the history of humanity realize that dream of the one shepherd and the one flock, *da nur ein Hirt und eine Herde stattfindet*. On the other hand, for Cohen the culmination of the history of religion would be in that day when God will be One. The truth of monotheism is incomparable and eternal; the future is the anticipation of the actualization and permeation of this truth. It may be said that the systematic development of Cohen's thought from the *Ethik* to the *Religion der Vernunft* is a commentary to his belief in monotheism and its implications. Totality and pureness are the guiding terms of his philosophy, be it expressed in logic, in ethics, or in aesthetics, just as skepticism, eudaemonism, and subjectivism were attitudes and positions that he rejected. He arrived at a philosophy of religion with Judaism at its center, but his philosophy and, in particular, his fundamental belief in reason made him an opponent of all those thought patterns that spelled the destruction for reason and subsequently for the Jew. We can speak of a Cohen *Weltanschauung*.

The study of the problem of the virtues in Kant's *Metaphysics of Morals and in* Cohen's *Ethik* and *Religion der Vernunft* helps us to trace a development that has led from a moral philosophy to a religious one and the changing role that the virtues play in them. From Kant's attitude that a virtue is a self-constraint that is rooted in inner freedom and is at the same time an awareness of a duty that is formal law, we conclude that man has an intelligible nature with a faculty of practical reason and is capable of freedom, i.e., the knowledge that his will is free. The moral universe, its being or nonbeing, was inseparable from man as the subect of morality. Cohen's doctrine of virtues was an elaborate commentary on Kant, and it was only in his further elaboration of the virtue of justice that Cohen advanced this Kantian discussion. But apart from significant shifts in position there is in Cohen that detail of evaluation of the history of thought in the nineteenth century that turns the whole problem of the virtues into a broad philosophic dialogue with all those movements that threatened to cast doubt upon reason and rational knowledge. The virtues are placed in the service of humanity. They are the ways that lead to the ideal, to *Sophrosyne*. It is this ideal of virtue that now stands in contradiction to philosophies of pessimism, of aphorism and atheism. The study of Cohen's thought cannot be isolated from the philosophies and styles that he passionately opposed. It is through these that we can penetrate the implications of Cohen's position. His thought is deepest at the moment when it is contradictory to Nietzsche's, to Schopenhauer's, or to Hegel's, for here even the world of contrasts is no longer applicable. The moral world in which Cohen believed was for him truth. Cohen's philosophy surpasses specific philosophic problems and involves an evaluation and a reconstruction of man's place and meaning in the universe.

Cohen's final work surpassed his attachment to Kant; the writing of a philosophy of religion from Jewish sources, and from the conviction that Israel was the embodiment of an eternal truth, the truth of monotheism, made it necessary for Cohen to think in terms of a metaphysics that Plato, Maimonides, and Leibniz—but not Kant—could inspire. In Israel past, present, and future, the divisions of historical time were transfigured in eternity. The messianic hope and the messianic peace that were now the supreme virtue were embodied in Israel's eternity. Her historical presence was the witness to a truth that the future was yet to reveal, but that Cohen believed the Jew embraced in the *Shabbath*, the Day of Atonement, the Passover, and in the cycle of the religious year. But is was under the Yoke of the Law, willingly accepted, that the Jew lived in the Kingdom of God, for it was in that kingdom that the holy was separated from the profane. The purity that had permeated all of Cohen's works were symbolized in the Israel that bore within it the verity of verities. Israel was for Cohen that symbol of truth which fills all life from thought to ethics to beauty. The virtues were no longer ideals, but preparations to servanthood, the goal of the universe God had determined in creation and in revelation; man was no longer the center of value, but in correlation became a co-worker, a suffering servant on behalf of God. The days of the Messiah would bring a knowledge of God, men would destroy injustice, and the ethical realm—distant as it now is from the divine—would be transformed into a messianic one. The ethical realm, reflecting the mutual obligations among men, is validated no longer from within but from divine command. God's oneness will encompass all realms. Israel suffers martyrdom of this monotheism. What is deepest in Cohen is the rejection of the Christian doctrine of sin and grace, that separation between salvation and damnation. Israel is the spiritual and physical redemption of man and the world; evil and death point only to our inadequate and insufficient knowledge, the yet incomplete relationship between monotheism and the world. In repentance there is redemption; in humility, the virtue which for Cohen has no limits, the moral quality of the world is born. Sin does not invalidate man's moral obligation. Cohen rewrote his *Ethik* in terms of piety and humility, virtues that he had previously ignored or did not esteem, but that he now highly valued. God is truth, and it is in the knowledge of this truth that piety and humility find their source. Israel was for Cohen the collective name for the pious of the world.

If we consider the change in direction of Cohen's last book we may say that in a significant way the domination of Kant's metaphysical ethics was weakened. Cohen wrote a theodicy of monotheism; Judaism was its monadic receptacle. He believed, therefore, that Christianity and all other previous religions could but be preparatory to Judaism's truth. Contrary to almost all historical schemes that might end with the euthanasia of Judaism, Cohen saw Judaism as the eternal truth and center from which the others radiated, and their distance, i.e., their separation, from this center endangered the pureness of Israel's faith. The concrete expression of this pureness was the messianic peace; it was the peace of the *Shabbath* with its further political, social, and economic consequences. The way from *Sophrosyne* to *Shalom* delineated the development of Cohen's thought from the *Ethik* to the *Religion der Vernunft*.

Before Cohen's death in 1918 two significant works in the philosophy of religion had appeared. No consideration of Cohen's achievements would be adequate unless they are seen in relation to Ernst Troeltsch's *Die Soziallehren der Christlichen Kirchen und Gruppen* (1911) and Rudolf Otto's *Das Heilige* (1917). It is to Troeltsch's work that we first turn our attention.

The problem for Troeltsch is to reconcile the historical evolution of Christian thought and teaching with the great moments of religious life, e.g., Jesus, Paul, Luther, *inter alia*. The Christian message of the Kingdom of God proclaimed by Jesus must be comprised with the world; it is this confrontation of the Kingdom and the world that constitutes the source of the social teaching of the Christian churches.[1] The study of the history of Christian thought is rooted not only in compromise with economic, social, and political realities, but in the opposition to this compromise which emerges from the *a priori* nature of the religious.[2] To the

[1] Ernst Troeltsch, *The Social Teaching of the Christian Churches*, trans. O. Wyon (London, 1931), p. 999. "On the one hand it [the Ethos of the Gospel] demands the sanctification of the self for God. . . . One the other hand, it demands brotherly love, which overcomes in God all the tension and harshness of the struggle for existence. . . . This is an ideal which requires a new world if it is to be fully realized. . . . But it is an ideal which cannot be realized within this world apart from compromise. Therefore the history of the Christian Ethos becomes the story of a constantly renewed search for this compromise, and of fresh opposition to this spirit of compromise."

[2] Troeltsch, "Das religioese Apriori" (1909), in *Gesammelte Schriften*, II (Tuebingen, 1922), 754–68.

Kantian theoretical, moral, and aesthetic *a priori* Troeltsch added a religious *a priori*, a point of contact between man and God that allows us to say: "The truth is—and this is the conclusion of the whole matter—the Kingdom of God is within us."[3] Although Troeltsch recognizes a religious *a priori*, a *Vernunftgesetz*, and an *immanentes Notwendigkeits- und Verpflichtungsgefuehl*, he refuses to concede the possibility of an "ethical transformation of material nature or of human nature."[4] The problem is without resolution; every religious life expression belongs to historical evolution. The finite and the infinite are identical; each historical moment of religious life is an incarnation of the infinite spirit. There can be no absolute Christian ethic; only the incarnated spirit is absolute.[5] In agreement, therefore, with Ranke, Troeltsch believed that each historical period "exists directly for God"; each is unique in that it embodies the contingent and the irrational. To explore the contingency and irrationality of historical evolution is to stand open to the ongoing revelation which is both immanent and transcendent in each incarnated moment.[6] Troeltsch realized the uniqueness of each historical moment of religious life, the sum of which corresponded to the divine life. This divine life is greater than all its moments, and man is driven from the inadequacy of each to transcend not only the various stages of religious experience, but in faith and trust to confront the continuing revelatory power of the Divine Spirit. This leads to what Troeltsch would call "natural motives for heroism."[7] With this deepening absorption of revelation and its transformation by political, social, and economic forces, there arises at the same time a liberation of the Spirit, an asceticism challenging the deadening affects of the finite. It is this asceticism that characterizes the Kingdom in man, the religious *a priori*, and it is this inner Kingdom that must be eternally awakened and freed from the historical existence, for

[3] *Social Teaching of the Christian Churches*, p. 1013.

[4] Ibid.

[5] T. K. Oesterreich, *Die deutsche Philosophie des XIX. Jahrhunderts und der Gegenwart* (Basel, 1951), p. 603: "Die Monade bedeutet die Identitaet des endlichen und unendlichen Geistes bei Aufrechterhaltung der Endlichkeit und Individualitaet des letzteren." Oesterreich is quoting Troeltsch's *Historicism and Its Problems*, vol. III, *G. S.*

[6] Troeltsch, "Moderne Geschichtsphilosophie" (1904), *G.S.*, II, 673–728. "Sie rationalisiert die Historie nicht zur Exekution eines allgemeinen Begriffes, sondern laesst die Irrationalitaet aller individuellen Bildungen bestehen, indem sie den individuellen Charakter jeder solchen Metaphysik selbst anerkennt. Sie wird dadurch dann aber doch nicht zu einer bloss subjektiven Meinung, sondern, indem sie aus gewissenhafter Versenkung in die Historie und aus der Deutung ihres Sinnes hervorgeht, sucht dieses Urteil die Kontinuitaet und bildet es sie weiter als eine relativ schoepferische Tat" (p. 727).

[7] Troeltsch, *The Social Teaching*, pp. 1005–6: "The idea of the future Kingdom of God . . . does not render this world and life in this world meaningless and empty; on the contrary, it stimulates human energies, making the soul strong . . . in the certainty of an ultimate, absolute meaning and aim for human labor. . . . This idea . . . is the only means by which strength and heroism may be maintained in a general spiritual situation."

in its freedom lies the essence of its message.[8]

In the concept of contingency Troeltsch points to the hopelessness of all philosophical and theological attempts to find categories by which the free creative activity of the Divine can be comprehended. In this he rejects the Panlogism of Hegel and the theosophy of Schelling and is forced into an antinomic position. The consequences, however, of absolute irrationalism and absolute rationalism are impossible: the first leads to the incoherence and violence of all things, the second to a pantheism which is ethically untenable in terms of the obvious separation between the what *is* and the what *should be*. Troeltsch believes that each assumed position—be it theistic, anti-theistic, pantheistic, or nominalistic-empirical—bears contradictions and incoherencies.[9] But if all religious life is permeated with contradictions, then no ideals can be realized, for "they will meet the fate which always awaits every fresh creation of religious and ethical thought; they will render indispensable services and they will develop profound energies, but they will never fully realize their actual intention within the sphere of our earthly struggle and conflict."[10] It is Troeltsch's great sensitivity to the interplay of the eternal and the temporal that makes him aware of the demonic danger that lies in all attempts to realize within the temporal an eternal truth. Each compromise is the result of the barrier of "brutal fact" and the "interior and exterior difficulties" that oppose the Kingdom of God. It is the struggle against the claims of the final synthesis, the reconciliation of mind and matter, body and soul, the eternal and temporal, that forces Troeltsch to declare that "the final ends of all humanity are hidden within His Hands."[11] This for Troeltsch is not a matter of resignation, but the imposition of the historical demand to force open each closing synthesis, to reveal its inadequacies and insufficiencies, and above all to know that revelation is incomplete and that new categories and new structures of thought will be needed and will evolve to meet the new dimensions of divine revelations. The history of religion is thus the constant and unceasing confrontation between the world and the logos.[12]

[8] Troeltsch, "Was heisst Wesen des Christentums?" (1903), *G.S.*, II, 386–451. Troeltsch here summarizes the method of this research. "So wird man fuer die rein empirisch-historische Darstellung auch nach einem die Moeglichkeiten und Komplikationen in sich schliessenden Wesensund Entwicklungsbegriff suchen muessen" (p. 449).

[9] Troeltsch, "Contingency," *Encyclopedia of Religion and Ethics*, ed. J. Hastings (New York, 1951), p. 89: "Absolute Rationalism, with Pantheism as its logical conclusion, and absolute Irrationalism, with its logical consequences of the irrelation and incoherence of things, or Polytheism, are alike impossible. . . . The actual thinking activity of man consists in a continuous combination of the antitheses."

[10] Troeltsch, *Social Teaching*, p. 1013.

[11] Ibid.

[12] Troeltsch, "Die Zukunftsmoeglichkeiten des Christentums im Verhaeltnis zur modernen Philosophie" (1910), *G.S.*, II, 862: "Nennt man die Zustimmung zu der Grundvoraussetzung dieser Systeme ein Bekenntnis zum Logos und zu seiner Herrschaft ueber die von ihm

If we ask about the relationship between Cohen and Troeltsch, it would seem that on the basis of a preliminary comparison there is little. The ethical substance of Judaism expressed in the uniqueness of monotheism has no parallel in Troeltsch's concept of the Kingdom. Israel is for Cohen a moral and religious absolute, and those who dwell within her live the eternity of truth. In Israel, Rationalism and Irrationalism are transcended. Israel is the Kingdom. Cohen refuses the historicism of Troeltsch; it is overcome in the messianic meaning of Israel. Troeltsch and Cohen join in their anticipation of the future, their belief in the further revelation of the truth of the Kingdom or the messianic age. There is a profound belief in the religious evolution of man, and the realization that perhaps the history of religion in its theistic and messianic implications has only just begun. This is the natural motive for heroism that Troeltsch had spoken of, a standing open to stages of the religious life which the future may yet reveal. The Jew is the martyr of monotheism and has suffered the martyrdom; symbolically and historically the fact of Israel is the primordial expression of the truth of the martyrdom. Historicism could play no role in Cohen's thought.

"Before God." These words are for Cohen expressive of the sanctifying and redeeming reality of monotheism, but these words reveal also a *mysterium tremendum et fascinosum*, and it is to this experience that Rudolf Otto has made a significant contribution. If we are to give further meaning to the term *correlation*, the work of Otto becomes helpful. He introduces such terms as *numen praesens* and creature-feeling into the divine–human correspondence, while eliminating all possibilities of conceptual explanations.[13] In fact, the introduction of this terminology all indicative of "the feeling of a numinous object objectively given" is descriptive of a primary datum of consciousness;[14] the "feeling of dependence" is a consequence.

---

gedachte und gestaltete Welt, dann ist der Glaube an die israelitisch-christliche religioese Lebenswelt zugleich ein Glaube an den Logos, und es wird klar, wie heutige Christentum sich trotz aller Unterschiede mit dem alten darin verbindet, dass der Glaube an Gott in Christus zusammernschmilzt mit dem Glauben an den Logos in der Welt." For an evaluation of Troeltsch's influence on comtemporary theology, see the remarks in Paul Tillich, *Perspectives in 19th and 20th Century Protestant Theology* (New York, 1967), pp. 230–34.

[13] Rudolph Otto, *The Idea of the Holy* (New York, 1967), pp. 9–10. When Abraham ventures to plead with God for the men of Sodom, he says: Behold now I have taken upon me to speak unto the Lord, which am but dust and ashes (Gen.18:27). "There you have," Otto explains, "something other than, *merely* a feeling of dependence. Desiring to give it a name of its own, I propose to call it 'creature-consciousness' or 'creature-feeling.' It is the emotion of creature, submerged and overwhelmed by its own nothingness in contrast to that which is supreme above all creatures."

[14] Ibid., see p. 11n. With Otto's terms we can more clearly understand the implications of Kant's discussion of the sublime: "The sublime is that in comparison with which everything else is small." In fact, Otto's work is a significant consequence of the implications of Kant's concept of the sublime.

The three central terms in Otto's analysis are *Tremendum*, *Mysterium*, and *Fascinosum*. With all these terms we enter the world of feeling, and in a Kantian sense we are closest to the feeling of the sublime. It is in this realm that Otto discovers the religious, and in his comparative study of mysticism he demonstrates the universality of the feeling and shows that the same primal impulses dominate the mystic, be he from East or from West. What must always be explored and analyzed are the similarities that constitute these primal impulses.[15] Illustrative of the religious feeling of the *tremendum* are the elements of "overpoweringness," *das Ungeheuere*, and "absolute unapproachability." This, however, does not lead to the naught of self or the "consciousness of absolute dependence" in a Schleiermacher sense. We start in Otto's words "from a consciousness of the absolute superiority and supremacy of the power other than myself, and it is only as it falls back upon ontological terms to achieve its end . . . that that element of the *tremendum*, originally apprehended as 'plenitude of power,' becomes transmuted into 'plenitude of being.'"[16] Here the difference between createdness or *Geschaffenheit* and creaturehood or *Geschoepflichkeit* is vital. We distinguish here first between the Schleiermacher "feeling of dependence" and Abraham's "creature-consciousness." For Abraham, the category of the numinous "does involve the littleness of every creature in face of that which is above all creatures"; the "feeling of our createdness," on the other hand, assumes a causal relation between God and the creature and thus a "consciousness of absolute dependence" and stress upon the reality of self.[17] This latter feeling is conceptual and therefore explains the religious to a lesser degree than does creaturehood. The religious problem is creature-consciousness.

From the *tremendum* Otto turns to an analysis of the *mysterium*.

[15] Rudolph Otto, *Mysticism East and West* (New York, 1959), p. xvi: "We maintain that in mysticism there are indeed strong primal impulses working in the human soul which as such are completely unaffected by differences of climate, of geographical position or of race." See also Otto, *The Idea of the Holy*, p. 112. The holy is an *a priori* category: "We conclude then that not only the rational but also the non-rational elements of the complex category of "holiness" are *a priori* elements and each in the same degree. Religion is not in vassalage either to morality or teleology, *ethos* or *telos*, and does not draw its life from postulates; and its non-rational content has, no less than its rational, its own independent root in the hidden depth of the spirit itself." These remarks of Otto show that in reference to the religious Cohen's point of departure, the ethical, is shunted aside for a pure phenomenological investigation. No such path could be possible to Cohen, who realized in correlation the ethical transfiguration of both man and mankind. All other religious phenomena should be descriptive of this primal *ethos* and *telos*.

[16] *The Idea of the Holy*, p. 21.

[17] Ibid., p. 22: "But essentially mysticism is the stressing to a very high degree, indeed the overstressing, of the non-rational or supra-rational elements in religion . . . a feeling of our creaturehood."

He defines the *mysterium* as the "wholly other, that which is quite beyond the sphere of the usual, the intelligible, and the familiar . . . filling the mind with blank wonder and astonishment."[18] The "wholly other" is contrasted not only with nature, with being, and with all that "is"; it becomes "that which is nothing."[19] The mystics have made us aware of the uniqueness of the "wholly other" reality and quality of the divine, and it is in this sense that such terms as *supernatural* and *transcendent* convey in a "positive feeling-content" that which the "wholly other" seems to imply only in a negative sense. The nonrational content of religion of which the mysterious is but one element can free the religious from subservience to rational conception, given in ethics and Messianism. Otto affirmed that no vassalage to such conceptualization can be admitted for the religious. However, in terms of the mysterious object there is numbing, for the object is beyond comprehension and within this experience ethics is of no significance.[20] Otto points to these nonrational elements to illustrate his belief that religion subordinated to ethics and teleology is incomplete and indeed violated.

The third fundamental element of the numinous experience is that of fascination. The numinous "shows itself as something uniquely attractive and fascinating."[21] The numinous as mystery is not only an object of wonder, but it entrances, bewilders, confounds, captivates, and transports with a strange ravishment.[22] Otto explains that there is a longing to possess the *numen* for its own sake, and this does not involve a utilitarian aim. This longing, however, does seek the aid of the numinous for results in the natural world. This longing arises from "independent roots in the hidden depth of the spirit"; we can call this longing, primal. The study of religion is for Otto a search for "the qualitative content of the numinous experience." Fascination is present not only in the religious feeling of longing, but in the moment of "solemnity."[23] It would appear that the

[18] Ibid., p. 26.

[19] Ibid., p. 30: ". . . in fact the void of the eastern, like the 'nothing' of the western, mystic is a numinous ideogram of the 'wholly other.'"

[20] Ibid., p. 28: "The truly 'mysterious' object is beyond our apprehension and comprehension, not only because our knowledge has certain irrevocable limits, but because in it we come upon something inherently 'wholly other,' whose kind and character are incommensurable with our own, and before which we therefore recoil in a wonder that strikes us chill and numb."

[21] Ibid, p. 30.

[22] Ibid.: "The 'mystery' is for him not merely something to be wondered at but something that entrances him; and beside that in it which bewilders and confounds, he feels a something that captivates and transports him with a strange ravishment, rising often enough to the pitch of dizzy intoxication. . . ."

[23] Ibid., p. 35: "it is already alive and present in the moment of solemnity, both in the gathered concentration and humble submergence of private devotion, when the mind is exalted to the holy, and in the common worship of the congregation, where this is practiced with earnestness and deep sincerity."

deepest moments of the religious lie beyond the rational in the "ultimate and highest part of our soul." For Otto, Kant's attempt to construct "a religion within the limits of reason alone" could be possible only if what he has called the "independent roots" can be ignored. The religious can be understood only in terms of what it is in "its own essential nature," and this nature Otto has defined as the *mysterium tremendum et fascinosum*. But this *mysterium tremendum* brings forth in the creature an "unutterableness" of what is experienced. This "unutterableness" Otto tells us is confirmed by the "converted from St. Paul onward." Otto is a seeker of the religious "predisposition" and its transformation into a "driving impulsion."[24]

Perhaps more serious for Cohen is Otto's rejection of a religious "vassalage to ethics." The ethical content, its messianic hope, the meaning and significance of monotheism are perhaps the sublimest aspects of a religious experience that has evolved with the history of man. The experience of the numinous is in Cohen's thought the ethical. The reality of the *mysterium tremendum* can also be ethical, and perhaps when it is, its consequences for humanity are most sublime and "unutterable," realizing a fascination that is beyond conceptual language. Protestant thought, too, easily sacrifices the ethical. In Troeltsch we are made deeply aware of the historical and the inadequacy and contingency of all religious manifestations, while after Otto no analysis of the *vita religiosa* is possible without the *mysterium tremendum et fascinosum*. But the correlation between man and God is rooted in His Holiness and our responsibility to become holy; it is rooted in the ethical substance of the divine–human correspondence. Without the concept of correlation the religious is too easily captured by either the descriptive methodology of Otto or the historicism of Troeltsch. The mediation of Law, Peoplehood, and Messianism reconciles for Cohen the awe of the Divine with the moral imperative. The liberation of man from servility to moral relativism depends upon a faith which is both philosophical and moral in a God who is the source of reason, value, and purpose.

[24] Ibid., p. 116: "It begins in undirected, groping emotion, a seeking and shaping of representations, and goes on, by a continual onward striving, to generate ideas, till its nature is self-illumined and made clear by an explication of the obscure *a priori* foundation of thought itself, out of which it originated."

BIBLIOGRAPHY

A. Primary Sources

Cohen, Hermann. *Ethik des reinen Willens.* 1907; 3d ed., Berlin, 1921. new ed. Hildesheim, 1981.

———. *Logik der reinen Erkenntnis.* 1902; 1914; 3d ed., Berlin, 1922; new ed. Hildesheim, 1977.

———. *Aesthetik des reinen Gefuehls.* Berlin, 1912.

———. *Kants Begruendung der Ethik.* 1877; 2d ed., Berlin, 1910.

———. *Kants Theorie der Erfahrung.* 1871; 1885; 3d ed., Berlin, 1918.

———. *Kants Begruendung der Aesthetik.* Berlin, 1889.

———. *Der Begriff der Religion im System der Philosophie.* Giessen, 1915.

———. *Religion der Vernunft aus den Quellen des Judentums.* 1919; 2d ed., Frankfurt am Main, 1929.

———. *Juedische Schriften.* 3 vols. Berlin, 1924.

———. *Schriften zur Philosophie und Zeitgeschichte.* 2 vols. Berlin, 1928. Contains the extremely important book *Das Prinzip der Infinitesimal-Methode und seine Geschichte: Ein Kapitel zur Grundlegung der Erkenntniskritik.* Berlin, 1883.

———. *Briefe.* Ed. Bertha Strauss and Bruno Strauss. Berlin, 1939.

Kant, Immanuel. *Werke.* Ed. W. Weischedel. 6 vols. Frankfurt am Main, 1964.

Translations

Jospe, Eva. *Hermann Cohen: Reason and Hope.* New York, 1971.

Kaplan, Simon. "The Day of Atonement." Chap. XII of Hermann Cohen's *Religion of Reason in Judaism.* Summer 1968, Winter 1969, Spring 1969.

———. *Hermann Cohen: Religion of Reason Out of the Sources of Judaism.* New York, 1972.

B. Secondary Sources

Agus, Jacob. *Modern Philosophies of Judaism.* New York, 1941.

Altmann, Alexander. “Theology in Twentieth Century Jewry.” *Leo Baeck Institute Year Book*, I. London, 1956.

_________. “Hermann Cohen Begriff der Korrelation.” In *In zwei Welten: Festchrift Siegfried Moses*. Tel-Aviv, 1962.

_________. “Zur Auseinendersetzung mit der dialektische Theologie.” *Monatsschrift fuer Geschichte und Wissenschaft des Judentums*, Jahrgang 79. Frankfurt am Main, 1935.

_________, ed. *Studies in Nineteenth Century Jewish Intellectual History*. Cambridge, 1964.

Barth, H. *Philosophie der praktischen Vernunft*. Tuebingen, 1927.

Baumgarten, David. “Unverschuldete Verschollenheit und unverdienter Ruhm.” In *Robert Weltsch zum 70. Geburtstag*. Tel-Aviv, 1961.

Bergman, S. Hugo. *Faith and Reason*. Washington, 1961.

_________. “Israel and the Oikoumene.” In *Studies in Rationalism, Judaism and Universalism, in Memory of Leon Roth*. London, 1966.

Blumenberg, Hans. “Kant und die Frage nach dem ‘gnadigen Gott.’” *Studium Generale*, VII (1954), 9.

Bornhausen, Karl. “Das Problem der Wirklichkeit Gottes.” *Festgabe fuer W. Hermann*. Tuebingen, 1917.

_________. “Die Religion der Vernunft.” *Kantstudien*, 1924.

Cassirer, Ernst. “Hermann Cohen und die Erneuerung der Kantischen Philosophie.” *Kantstudien*, XVII, 1912.

_________. *Myth of the State*. New Haven, 1946.

_________. *The Philosophy of Symbolic Forms*. Vol. III. New Haven, 1957.

_________. “Hermann Cohen: Worte gesprochen an seinem Grab.” *Neue Juedische Monatshefte*. Berlin, 1918.

_________. “Hermann Cohen.” Vortrag. *Korrespondenzblatt*. Frankfurt am Main, 1920. Vol. I, *Des Vereins zur Gruendung und Erhaltung einer Akademie des Judentums*.

Dussort, Henri. *L'Ecole de Marbourg*. Paris, 1963.

Ebbinghaus, J. “Deutschtum und Judentum bei Hermann Cohen.” *Kantstudien*, 60. Jahrgang, Heft I, 1969.

Fackenheim, Emil L. “Hermann Cohen: After Fifty Years.” *Leo Baeck Memorial Lecture*, No. 12. New York, 1969.

Frank, Erich. “Knowledge, Will and Belief.” In *Collected Essays*. Ed. Ludwig Edelstein. Zurich, 1955.

_________. *Philosophical Understanding and Religious Truth*. London, 1945.

Fritzsche, Robert A. *Hermann Cohen aus persoenlicher Erinnerung*. Berlin, 1922.

Gawronsky, Dimitry. “Ernst Cassirer: His Life and His Work.” In *The Philosophie of Ernst Cassirer*. Evanston, 1949.

Goerland, Albert. "Hermann Cohens systematische Arbeit im Dienste des kritischen Idealismus." *Kantstudien*, XVII, 1912.

Goldstein, Walter. *Hermann Cohen*. Jerusalem, 1963.

Graupe, Heinz. *Die Stellung der Religion im Systematischen der Marburger Schule*. Berlin, 1930.

Gregor, M. J. *Laws of Freedom*. Oxford, 1963.

Gruenewald, P. P. *Hermann Cohen*. Hanover, 1968.

Guttmann, Julius. *Die Philosophie des Judentums*. Munich, 1933. English ed., *Philosophies of Judaism*. Introd. by R. J. Zwi Werblowsky. New York, 1964.

————. "Religion und Wissenschaft im mittelalterlichen und modernen Denken." *Festschrift zum 50-jaehrigen Bestehen der Hochschule fuer die Wissenschaft des Judentums*. Berlin, 1922.

Heinemann, Fritz. *Die Philosophie im 20. Jahrhundert*. Stuttgart, 1963.

Henrich, Dieter. *Der ontologische Gottesbeweis*. Tuebingen, 1960.

Herrmann, Wilhelm. "Hermann Cohens Ethik." *Christliche Welt*. Marburg i. H., 1907.

Judaica: Festschrift zu Hermann Cohens 70. Geburstag, von Elbogen, Kellermann, Mittwoch. Berlin, 1912.

Kaplan, Simon. *Das Geschichtsproblem in der Philosophie Hermann Cohen*. Berlin, 1930.

Kaufmann, Erich. *Kritik der Neukantischen Rechtsphilosophie*. Aalen, 1964.

Kinkel, Walter. *Hermann Cohen*. Stuttgart, 1924.

————. "Das Urteil des Ursprungs." *Kantstudien*, XVII, 1912.

Klatzkin, Jacob. *Hermann Cohen*. Berlin, 1921.

Krueger, Gerhard. *Philosophie und Moral in der Kantischen Kritik*. Tuebingen, 1967.

Liebeschuetz, Hans. "Hermann Cohen and His Historical Background." *Leo Baeck Institute Year Book*, XIII. London, 1968.

————. "Jewish Thought and Its German Background." *Leo Baeck Institute Year Book*, I. London, 1956.

————. "Hermann Cohen und Spinoza." *Bulletin, Leo Baeck Institute*, 12. Tel-Aviv, 1960.

Lewkowitz, Albert. "Religion und Philosophie im juedischen Denken der Gegenwart." *Monatsschrift fuer Geschichte und Wissenschaft des Judentums*, Jahrgang 79. Breslau, 1935.

Lisser, Kurt. *Der Begriff des Rechts bei Kant: Mit einem Anhang ueber Cohen und Coerland*. Berlin, 1922.

Loewith, Karl. "Philosophie der Vernunft und Religion der Offenbarung." *Neue Rundschau*, 79. Jahrgang (1968), Viertes Heft.

Marburg: Bild einer alten Stadt: Impressionen und Profile. Honnef/Rhein, 1961. Remembrances of Cohen by Boris Pasternak and Jose Ortega y Gasset.

Natorp, Paul. *Hermann Cohen als Mensch, Lehrer und Forscher: Gedaechtnisrede*, gehalten in der Aula der Universitaet Marburg. Marburg, 1918.

_________. *Hermann Cohens philosophische Leistung*. Berlin, 1918.

Otto, Rudolf. *The Idea of the Holy*. London, 1967.

_________. *Verantwortliche Lebensgestaltung*. Metta Kinau Verlag Zuneberg.

Philosophische Abhandlungen: H. Cohen zum 70. Geburtstag dargebracht. Berlin, 1912.

Riegner, Heinrich. "Hermann Cohen: Der Mensch." *Bulletin, Leo Baeck Institute*, No. 7. Tel-Aviv, 1959.

Ritzel, Wolfgang. *Studien zum Wandel der Kantauffassung*. Meisenheim, Glan, 1952.

Rosenzweig, Franz. *Kleinere Schriften*. Berlin, 1937. See the following articles: "Hermann Cohens Juedische Schriften"; "Hermann Cohens Nachlasswerk"; "Vertauschte Fronten."

_________. *Briefe*. Berlin, 1935.

Rotenstreich, Nathan. *The Recurring Pattern: Studies in Antijudaism in Modern Thought*. London, 1963.

_________. *Spirit and Man*. The Hague, 1963.

_________. *Jewish Philosophy in Modern Times*. New York, 1968.

Scholem, Gershom. *Judaica*. Frankfurt am Main, 1963.

Scholz, Heinrich. *Religionsphilosophie*. Berlin, 1921.

Schwarzschild, Steven S. "Introduction" to new edition of Hermann Cohen, *Ethik des reinen Willens*, Hildesheim, 1981.

Schweitzer, Albert. *Die Religionsphilosophie Kant von der Kritik der reinen Vernunft bis zur Religion innerhalb der Grenzen der blossen Vernunft*. Tuebingen, 1899.

Simon, Ernst. "Zu Hermann Cohens Spinoza: Auffassung." *Monatsschrift fuer Geschichte und Wissenschaft des Judentums*, Jahrgang 79. Breslau, 1935.

Slonimsky, Henry. "Hermann Cohen." *Historia Judaica*, IV, No. 2 (1942).

Solowiejczyk, Joseph. *Das reine Denken und die Seinskonstituierung bei Hermann Cohen*. Berlin, 1933.

Sonderheft der Neuen Juedischen Monatshefte: Zur Erinnerung an Hermann Cohen. Contributions by Cassirer, Natorp, Klatzkin, Kellermann, Joel, Rosenzweig, and B. Strauss. 1917–18.

Troeltsch, Ernst. *The Social Teaching of the Christian Churches*. Trans. O. Wyon. London, 1931.

_________. *Gesammelte Schriften*. Vol. II. Tuebingen, 1922.

_________. "Das Historische in Kants Religionsphilosophie." *Kantstudien*, IX, 1904.

Ueberwegs, Friedrich. *Grundriss der Geschichte der Philosophie*. Vol. IV, *Die deutsche Philosophie des XIX. Jahrhunderts und der Gegenwart*. Basel, 1951.

Ucko, Siegfried. *Der Gottesbegriff in der Philosophie Hermann Cohens*. Berlin, 1929.

Vuillemin, Jules. *L'Héritage kantien et la révolution copernicienne*. Paris, 1954.

Weil, Eric. *Problèmes kantiens*. Paris, 1963.

Weltsch, Robert. *Introduction to Leo Baeck Institute Year Book*, XIII. London, 1968.

Weyand, Klaus. *Kants Geschichtsphilosophie*. Cologne, 1963.

Wiener, Max. "Begriff und Aufgabe der Juedischen Theologie." *Monatsschrift fuer Geschichte und Wissenschaft des Judentums*, Jahrgang 77. Breslau, 1933.

Zwiezynski, Chiel. "Hermann Cohen (1842–1918): Erinnerung und Wuerdigung." *Tradition und Erneuerung: Zeitschrift der Vereinigung fuer religioesliberales Judentum in der Schweiz*, 18. St. Gallen, 1964.

INDEX

HIEBERT LIBRARY
3 6877 00003 6417